Alfred North Whitehead

Twayne's English Authors Series

Kinley E. Roby, Editor
Northeastern University

TEAS 374

ALFRED NORTH WHITEHEAD
(1861–1947)
Photograph courtesy of
Harvard University Archives

Alfred North Whitehead

By Paul Grimley Kuntz

Emory University

Twayne Publishers • *Boston*

Alfred North Whitehead

Paul Grimley Kuntz

Copyright © 1984 by G.K. Hall & Company
All Rights Reserved
Published by Twayne Publishers
A Division of G. K. Hall & Company
70 Lincoln Street
Boston, Massachusetts 02111

Book Production by Marne B. Sultz

Book Design by Barbara Anderson

Printed on permanent/durable acid-free
paper and bound in the United States of
America.

Library of Congress Cataloging in Publication Data

Kuntz, Paul Grimley, 1915–
  Alfred North Whitehead.

  (Twayne's English authors series ; TEAS 374)
  Bibliography: p. 150
  Includes index.
  1. Whitehead, Alfred North, 1861–1947.
I. Title.   II. Series
B1674.W354K86   1984   192   83-12999
ISBN 0-8057-6860-2

For Marion
who shows great love for all our children—
Charles, Alan, Sarah, Joel, Timothy, and Susan.

Contents

About the Author

Paul Grimley Kuntz, a Pennsylvanian, was born in Philadelphia and educated at Haverford College (B.A. 1937) and Harvard University (S.T.B. 1940, S.T.M. 1941, Ph.D. 1946). After first teaching at Smith College he spent eighteen years at Grinnell College. Since 1966 he has been Professor of Philosophy at Emory University.

His writings have included a coauthored *Philosophy: The Study of Alternative Beliefs, Lotze's System of Philosophy,* and *The Concept of Order,* in addition to about a hundred articles on order, with emphasis on medieval and American, metaphysics, philosophy of religion and aesthetics. Although he began with the hope of Whitehead and Russell in a purely formal definition of order, he has been changing to more concrete conceptions, as in the relation of man to the orders of nature. These studies were fostered by a Woodrow Wilson Fellowship at the Smithsonian Institution.

Kuntz's concern with order began as an undergraduate in the 1930s, when so many nations were experimenting with "new orders." The New Deal included then on the dollar bill the Great Seal's "novus ordo seclorum." A semester at Heidelberg University, then being politicized by the Nazis, gave Kuntz enough of "die neue Ordnung." His reaction was a story, published in 1936, with the moral that the new order was a new disorder (the title was "Ruhe und Unordnung").

During the 1970s Kuntz worked in close conjunction with his wife, Dr. Marion Leathers Kuntz. She is Head of the Department of Foreign Languages and Regents Professor of Greek and Latin at Georgia State University. Their work together includes organizing conferences on concepts of order at the Medieval Institute of Western Michigan University. Among the modes of order are "hierarchy," "harmony," "balance," "opposition" "analogy," and "truth."

The major points of Kuntz's philosophy are that history shows that order has been central to philosophies of East and West and that order is the master concept of reconstructed systematic philosophy.

Preface

Alfred North Whitehead's philosophical system is the most adequate metaphysical theory produced in the twentieth century. In an age that turns to the sciences as the source of *all* knowledge, and that rests wisdom upon *sheer* faith or desperate decision, Whitehead dares to defend speculative philosophy "as a method productive of important knowledge." Whitehead begins *Process and Reality* with a defense of metaphysics or systematic philosophy, which he defines: "Speculative Philosophy is the endeavor to frame a coherent, logical, necessary system of general ideas in terms of which every element of our experience can be interpreted."[1] Thereby our author rejects positivism that belittles any claim to know that does not come from the laboratory, and also he rejects existentialism, or at least that extreme form of the movement, which rejects the possibility of any evidence or any argument bearing on choice as a groundless act of faith. The significance of Whitehead is that in his system logic and science remain always relevant to concerns of concrete individuals in the unique situations of history. We need not be described as being of two cultures, without a common language, and without communication. Whitehead's system is such a language and such a mode of communication.

Whitehead's writing is as controversial as is his philosophy. There are still with us those who object to his coining of new terms, as did that self-confessed "old fogey" George Santayana. Some are "old-minded and know exactly what they think" and the old terms are inseparable from their thought. Whitehead is not one of them, but one, says Santayana, of the "honest groping philosophers [who] can't dissimulate . . . they are young-minded, and feel that what there is to discover must surely be something splendid."[2] Whitehead, the "young-minded" was seventy-seven; Santayana, "the old-minded" was seventy-five. Youth, Whitehead tells us, is not measured by length of years.

A many-sided system, developed in stages involving *Principia Mathematica* (with Bertrand Russell), the greatest work in logic since Aristotle's, and works in mathematical physics rivaling Einstein's, and works in system-building rivaling Kant's and Hegel's, cannot be presented in a brief essay. But one key term can be dealt with as it applies in history, logic, the sciences, art, religion, and political life; this is ORDER. By following the many meanings, and by asking how orders relate one to another, we may suggest the richness and the unity of Whitehead's thought. The common meaning of "order" is a relation of definite sort.[3]

My thanks are to Whitehead, whose last lectures and conversation I enjoyed at Harvard, to those who have told me more of him and his writings than I myself discovered, to the editor of this series, to my students who have read him with pleasure, to those excellent librarians who help me, but above all to my wife, Marion Leathers Kuntz, who has sustained me in this work and without whose inspiration it could not be.

My thanks are expressed to the Emory Research Committee, and to the American Council of Learned Societies, to the American Philosophical Society, and the Woodrow Wilson Center for Scholars for support. The manuscript was beautifully typed by Mrs. Rose Bode and Mrs. Pat Redford. For editorial assistance I am deeply indebted to Mr. Ron Hall and Mr. Jacob Ownesby. Advice about the interpretation has come from the deep knowledge of Paul Weiss, Charles Hartshorne, and George J. Allan. For proofreading, the author is deeply indebted to Mr. William Brooks and Mr. Stephen Keith; and for assistance in compiling and organizing the index, at the end of the long process of producing a small book, deep thanks to Miss Mary Ann Kontaratos.

Paul Grimley Kuntz

Emory University

Chronology

1861   15 February, Alfred North Whitehead born at Ramsgate on the Isle of Thanet, Kent, England, the son of the Reverend Alfred Whitehead, a headmaster recently ordained priest of the Church of England (later Vicar of St. Peter's, Canon of Canterbury Cathedral, Rural Dean, and Proctor in Convocation for the Diocese).

1875   Enters school at Sherborne, Dorsetshire, England (for what Whitehead characterizes as a perfectly classical education).

1879–1880   "Head of the School" and "Captain of the Games."

1880   Goes up to Trinity College, Cambridge, as Scholar.

1885   B.A., Trinity College and appointed fellow of Trinity College. Also appointed lecturer in applied mathematics and mechanics.

1887   M.A., Trinity College.

1890   Marries Evelyn Willoughby Wade, daughter of Captain A. Wade, Seaforth Highlanders.

1891–1898   Children born: North, 1891 (an unnamed second boy died at birth, 1892); Jessie, 1893; Eric Alfred, 1898. All served in World War I. The youngest child was shot down in March 1918. To him is dedicated *An Enquiry Concerning the Principles of Natural Knowledge,* 1919:

To
ERIC ALFRED WHITEHEAD
ROYAL FLYING CORPS
November 27, 1898 to March 13, 1918
Killed in action over the Forêt de Gobain
giving himself that the city of his vision
may not perish.
The music of his life was without discord,
perfect in its beauty.

1898   *A Treatise on Universal Algebra.*

1900   Attends, with Bertrand and Alys Russell, the First International Congress of Philosophy in Paris.

1903   Abandons plans for a second volume of his *Treatise on Universal Algebra* (Vol. I, 1898) and Russell abandons his plan for a second volume of *The Principles of Mathematics:* Whitehead and Russell decide to collaborate. Elected Fellow of the Royal Society (F.R.S.).

1905   D.Sc., Trinity College.

1910   *Principia Mathematica,* Volume One (Two in 1912, Three in 1913, and Fourth abandoned). After twenty-five years at Trinity College, resigns post of Senior Lecturer.

1911   Begins teaching at University College, London. Professor of Applied Mathematics at Imperial College of Science and Technology.

1914   Attends the First Congress of Mathematical Philosophy, Paris, and reads paper on the Relational Theory of Space.

1919   Senator (and 1921 dean of faculty of science) of the University of London. Tarner Lecturer (lectures published in the following year as *The Concept of Nature.*)

1920   D.Sc., Manchester University (the first of a half-dozen honorary degrees from institutions of England, Scotland, Canada, and the United States).

1922   *The Principles of Relativity with Applications to Physical Science.*

1924   Resigns professorship at London to take a five-year appointment at Harvard University.

1925   Lowell Lecturer; *Science and the Modern World.*

1926   Harvard University invites him to teach as long as he feels able. Lowell Lecturer; *Religion in the Making.*

1927   Barbour-Page Lecturer at the University of Virginia; *Symbolism, Its Meaning and Effect.*

1927–1928   Gifford Lecturer at University of Edinburgh on *Process and Reality* (published 1929).

1929   Louis Clark Vanuxem Lecturer, Princeton University, *The Function of Reason*.

1929–1930   Mary Flexner Lecturer at Bryn Mawr College. Lectures with others given earlier at Dartmouth College, and later as Davies Lecturer at Columbia, become *The Adventures of Ideas* (1933).

1931   Elected Fellow of the British Academy (F.B.A.).

1933   Lecturer, University of Chicago. These lectures published under the title *Nature and Life* and reprinted in *Modes of Thought*.

1937   Retires from teaching at Harvard.

1937–1938   Lecturer at Wellesley College. These lectures published as *Modes of Thought* (1938).

1941   Ingersoll Lecturer, Harvard University: published under title *Immortality. The Philosophy of Alfred North Whitehead,* The Library of Living Philosophers.

1945   Awarded Order of Merit.

1947   30 December, dies in Cambridge, Massachusetts.

Abbreviations

It has become common, almost standard, in the books about Whitehead, to abbreviate the titles, and we have continued the practice of citing these in the text. Care needs to be paid to the editions cited in this book, for there are nearly always English editions, and sometimes both American and English paperbacks, usually with different paginations. We list the works alphabetically, citing the paperback of *Aims of Education* because there is no other now available.

AE	*The Aims of Education* (New York: The New American Library, 1949).
AI	*Adventures of Ideas* (New York: Macmillan Company, 1933).
CN	*The Concept of Nature* (Cambridge: At the University Press, 1920).
ESP	*Essays in Science and Philosophy* (London: Rider and Company, 1948).
FR	*The Function of Reason* (Princeton, N.J.: Princeton University Press, 1929).
IM	*Introduction to Mathematics* (revised ed., New York: Oxford University Press, 1958).
MCMW	*On Mathematical Concepts of the Material World* in F. S. C. Northrop and Mason W. Gross, eds., *Alfred North Whitehead: An Anthology* (New York: Macmillan, 1953), pp. 11–82.
MT	*Modes of Thought* (New York: The Macmillan Company, 1938).
PM	*Principia Mathematica* (Cambridge: At the University Press, Vol. I, 1910; Vol. II, 1912; Vol. III, 1913; 2d ed., 1925-1927).

PNK   *An Enquiry Concerning the Principles of Natural Knowledge* (Cambridge: At the University Press, 2d ed., 1925).

PR   *Process and Reality* (New York: Macmillan Co., 1929).

R   *The Principle of Relativity* (Cambridge: At the University Press, 1922).

RM   *Religion in the Making* (New York: Macmillan Co., 1927).

S   *Symbolism, Its Meaning and Effect* (New York: Macmillan Company, 1927).

SMW   *Science and the Modern World* (New York: Macmillan Co., 1926).

UA   *Universal Algebra* (Cambridge: At the University Press, 1898).

Note: These abbreviations conform to the usage of *Process Studies*.

Chapter One

Whitehead on Life and Learning: The Discovery of Rhythm

Introduction to an Introduction

It might seem superfluous for anyone to write an introduction to Whitehead, and it is puzzling that so many are required. Whitehead himself wrote as many introductory books as there are major divisions of his philosophy. In his mathematical period, at the same time as *Principia Mathematica*, he wrote *An Introduction to Mathematics*. At the conclusion of his period of teaching science, during which he did *The Principles of Natural Knowledge, The Concept of Nature,* and *The Principle of Relativity,* he produced *Science and the Modern World.* If some of his advanced works in theory of knowledge are obscure, the common reader can turn to his short, lucid works *Symbolism* and *The Function of Reason.* Among his popular works are a philosophy of civilization in *Adventures of Ideas* (Parts 1 and 4) and *Religion in the Making.* Both these contain sketches of his cosmology, and the reader can grasp the main outlines of this vision, even if he is baffled by the technicalities of *Process and Reality.* Whitehead also summed up the practical implications of his vast and many-sided achievement in *Aims of Education, Modes of Thought,* and *Essays in Science and Philosophy.*

Why then is there demand for so many introductions to Whitehead? The reason is that some readers need to interpret him as the outcome of some historic philosophy more familiar to them, such as Plato's or Aristotle's. Other readers need the orientation to his type of system, commonly called "the philosophy of organism" or "process philosophy." Other readers need to see the side of his philosophy that touches some great concern of theirs—logic, or science, or art, or politics, or civilization, or religion. All of these approaches are justified and needed. But if all these kinds of introduction already exist, why is yet another interpretation needed?

This book on Whitehead differs from its predecessors by connecting his thought on his own life with its implications for education. And in the very basic concern with his and others' lives, there is to be discerned a basic and important order, the dialectical interplay between romance and precision, and the synthesis in general ideas. With order as the central theme, there is the deep influence upon mathematics of the ancient Greek founder of philosophy, Pythagoras. This historical approach provides a closer linking together of the mathematical and logical with natural science and a philosophy of man and society. Since the Pythagorean tradition stressed harmony in the cosmos and all of its aspects, the way is open to consider order as the category central to knowledge, actuality and possibility, civilization and theology.

Whitehead himself defines mathematics as a "science of order," defines knowledge as ordering, asserts that without order nothing can be real, and presents human endeavors as a response to transcendent order. Since Whitehead himself provides these somewhat fragmented clues to unity in his thought, this book is a sustained effort to make clear his philosophy as the discovery of the many orders that together are our cosmos.

The Cyclical Order of Rhythm

The common reader, who is neither mathematician nor physicist nor philosopher, may safely approach Whitehead as he characterizes his own education and writes about education in the twentieth century. By taking first the autobiographical essays he or she will come to be attracted to Whitehead as an adventurous mind and one who set romance as the first phase of the educational order.

Although education must be primarily self-education, Whitehead devotes far fewer pages to his own education than to the education of others.

Perhaps no philosopher communicates his life and learning more charmingly than Whitehead. The reading of his autobiographical essays should be coupled with the reading of his essays on education. Not only does his life concern learning, both as a student and a teacher, but his educational philosophy arises from personal experience. But no summary of his "Autobiographical Notes," "Memories," "The Education of an Englishman," or "England and the Narrow Seas" is sufficient to convey the important order that is made explicit in *The Aims of Education* and amplified by the essays of Part 3, "Education," that accompany Part 1, "Personal," which include the above-named four autobiographical sketches.[1]

The most evident order of life and learning is, in Whitehead's analysis, the cyclical order. In the crucial address "The Rhythm of Education," we are reminded that "Hegel was right when he analyzed progress into three stages, which he called Thesis, Antithesis, and Synthesis; though for the purpose of the application of his idea to educational theory I do not think that the names he gave are very happily suggestive. In relation to intellectual progress I would term them, the stage of *romance,* the stage of *precision,* and the stage of *generalization.*"[2]

This kind of order, opposition between two and overcoming opposition through a third, is of course of the family of methods among which the best known are Hegel's idealist dialectic and Marx's materialistic dialectic. But it is never by Whitehead either identified with, or contrasted to, theirs. The main point of difference is that for Whitehead the statement of the cyclical order of rhythms does not require a special logic. One can recognize opposition without suspending the law of contradiction or the law of excluded middle. That is, we need not reject the principles so called: not both can a thing be and not be (contradiction), and either it is or it isn't, in the same sense at the same time (excluded middle). With these truths one can still recognize that life and learning are complex, and require for successful advance contrasts that do not occur in such a simple serial ordering as the integers 1, 2, 3, etc. If only there were but one principle of order such as "greater than by one," then we should be led by reason to prefer some more traditional formalization. One such familiar notion is expressed, for example, by St. Augustine, that we should learn the elements of the alphabet, then syllables, then words, then sentences, etc. Whitehead was "challenging the adequacy of some principles by which the subjects for study are often classified in order" (*AE, 27*). Whitehead confronts the order from simple to complex and asks us whether in fact we do learn in this way. "It is not true that the easier subjects should precede the harder. On the contrary, some of the hardest must come first because nature so dictates, and because they are essential to life" (ibid.). Whitehead then likens the acquisition of spoken language, early in childhood, to a miracle. After spoken, the infant must acquire written language, "the correlation of sounds with shapes. Great heavens! Have our educationists gone mad? They are setting babbling mites of six years old to tasks which might daunt a sage after lifelong toil" (*AE, 28*).

Although there is something in the order of "necessary antecedence," such as learning integers before you can learn fractions, this too is in most general form, false. "You cannot read Homer before you can read; but many a child, and in ages past many a man, has sailed with Odysseus over the seas of Romance by the help of the spoken word of a mother, or of some wandering bard" (ibid.).

It is important to overcome such simple ordering, particularly "in the hands of dull people with a turn for organization," because the concept of "uniform steady advance undifferentiated by change of type or alteration of pace" is death to the production of creative persons (ibid.).

The notion of "stages" does introduce the time series. There must also be what we all know so well in nature, periodicity.

In *Introduction to Mathematics* we find a chapter, "Periodicity in Nature," stressing the occurrence of "successive events so analogous to each other that, without any straining of language, they may be termed recurrences of the same event." Not merely is there day and night, one rotation of the earth, but the seasons as earth revolves around the sun, and the phases of the moon. Whitehead reminds us that early man felt life "influenced by . . . moonlight," and still there are the tides of the sea.[3]

The observation of periodic events gives rise to the concept of the "uniform flow of time" (*IM.,* 125), for we fuse the varying length of time "into one coherent measure," always following the order of "A, B, C. . . , so that A came before B, and B before C. . . ." This is fundamental to existence. "Our bodily life is essentially periodic. It is dominated by the beatings of the heart, and the recurrence of breathing" (*IM.,* 122).

These cycles are produced by the recurrence of alternating states and are relatively consistent and stable. But life is less consistent than machinery and we do not look "to the doctors of medicine for the regulation of our clocks" (*IM.,* 124). One crucial point relevant to the order of education is that there must be resonance. Whitehead's analysis with applications is lucid.

Now, suppose we excite the vibrations of a body by a cause which is itself periodic; then, if the period of the cause is very nearly that of one of the periods of the body, that mode of vibration of the body is very violently excited; even though the magnitude of the exciting cause is small. The phenomenon is called "resonance." The reason is easy to understand. Any one wanting to upset a rocking stone will push "in tune" with the oscillations of the stone, so as always to secure a favorable moment for a push. If the pushes are out of tune, some increase the oscillations, but others check them. But when they are in tune, after a time all the pushes are favorable. The word "resonance" comes from considerations of sound: but the phenomenon extends far beyond the region of sound. The laws of absorption and emission of light depend on it, the "tuning" of receivers for wireless telegraphy, the comparative importance of the influences of planets on each other's motion, the danger of a suspension bridge as troops march over it in step, and the excessive vibrations of some ships, under the rhythmical beat of their machinery at certain speeds. This coincidence of periodicities may produce steady phenomena when there is a constant association of the two periodic events, or it may produce violent and sudden outbursts when the association is fortuitous and temporary. (*IM.,* 125–26)

Whitehead the teacher attempts to find the tone to which his reader, as his listener, can vibrate. Sometimes he deliberately says what is unexpected. The first page of *Science and the Modern World* ends, asking "whether the scientific mentality of the modern world . . . is not a successful example of . . . provincial limitation."[4] The end of "Immortality," applies to Christian creeds, philosophic thought, and logic itself: "The exactness is a fake."[5] There is even the dissonant suggestion that metaphysics is a "cock and bull story."[6] But usually Whitehead, as in the passage on resonance itself, is showing us a mind that responds to the periodicities, expresses the patterns of nature, and sets us in sympathetic vibration.

Romance, Precision, Generalization

Whitehead follows a pattern strikingly similar to that of Romance, Precision, and Generalization in his "Autobiographical Notes." The critical reader should note that the first stage Whitehead himself enjoyed came from "direct experience of physical surroundings." He responded to his schoolmaster father as a man of "personality" among other provincial leaders: "men with strong mutual antagonisms and intimate community of feeling. The vision was one source of my interest in history and in education." Canterbury Cathedral stirred him to imagine the murder of Thomas à Becket "on the very spot where [he] fell A.D. 1170" (*ESP,* 7–9). The reader should allow Whitehead to share with him the imaginative appeal of "Memories" and "The Education of an Englishman." If ever there was an emphasis on the immediate, it is here. Most of the passages deal with sight, but some with sound, as of "the magnificent bells of the big Abbey Church [of Sherborne in Dorsetshire], which were brought from Tournai by Henry VIII when he returned from the Field of the Cloth of Gold . . ." (*ESP,* 27). Good education, in summary, should have a strong aesthetic background.

The general point about education needing a first moment of Romance is clear. "This aesthetic background was an essential element in the education, explanatory alike of inertia and latent idealism. The education cannot be understood unless it is realized that it elucidated an ever-present dream world in our subconscious life" (*ESP,* 27).

What was good in Whitehead's own education, as he judged it, and generalizes to any education, is the balance of opposites. Education should have, he is saying, like England, two very different sides. On one side there are "the polar currents and Siberian winds . . . come down the North Sea"; on the other, "subtropical interludes of South Atlantic weather . . ." (*ESP,* 27). If there is warm Romance, there must be, as in geographic opposition, cold Precision. "On the intellectual side, my education . . . conformed to the normal standard of the time. Latin began at the age of ten years, and Greek at twelve. . . . Daily, up to the age of nineteen and a half years, some pages of Latin and Greek authors were construed, and their grammar examined. Before going to school pages of rules of Latin grammar could be repeated, all in Latin, and exemplified by quotations. The classical studies were interspersed with mathematics" (*ESP,* 9). The opposites requiring synthesis are freedom and discipline.

In the phase of Romance Whitehead noted a "latent idealism," by which he might have meant the continuity of nature and man. Certainly the poets he mentioned as being favorites, Wordsworth and Shelley, also had forms of Plato's doctrines of the soul and of ideas (*ESP,* 9). In the phase of Precision Whitehead noted the perception of likenesses and differences between ancient and modern life (*ESP,* 30).

Although the first two stages, Romance and Precision, have some relation to Hegel's "Thesis" and "Antithesis," they are not exactly contradictory in a logical sense. Rather they are "immediate cognisance of fact" and analysis of fact, or the contrast of emotional excitement to exact formulation and "systematic order" (*AE,* 29–30).

"The final stage of generalization is Hegel's synthesis. It is a return to romanticism with added advantage of classified ideas and relevant technique. It is the fruition which has been the goal of the precise training" (*AE,* 30).

"Generalization," presented as lectures, gives us "general ideas" (*AE,* 37). Therefore what Whitehead stresses in his own university experience was the spirit of generalization. Not only in lectures, which stress "general principles" (*AE,* 38), is this true but also in the Platonic method of dialogue, in which "everything was discussed, politics, religion, philosophy, literature" (*ESP,* 10). The general is what is common to such diverse fields.

Like Hegel's dialectic, the three stages of the dialectic are repeated. "Education should consist in a continual repetition of such cycles. Each lesson in its minor way should form an eddy cycle issuing in its own subordinate process. Longer periods should issue in definite attainments, which then form the starting ground for fresh cycles. We should banish the idea of a mythical, far-off end of education. The pupils must be continually enjoying some fruition and starting afresh . . ." (*AE*, 31).

Elements of Absolute Idealism

Whitehead learned to philosophize as a late Victorian in a period when the absolute idealism of Hegel appealed to the motive of seeing life whole. We have seen the method of resolving opposites into an inclusive unity. Although British philosophy was dominated by F. H. Bradley, Whitehead resisted Hegel's influence. There was more than one truth and one reality.

The one interrelated whole was called by the British Hegelians "the Absolute." Whitehead resisted the conclusion because of a corollary he regarded as a disaster, that is, the denial of the autonomous reality of individual things. The doctrine of the Absolute implied also that nothing could be known unless everything is known, since nothing is except as related to everything, and what can be known is being or reality, which is the whole.

Because the idealists sought to relate anything whatsoever to everything and to discover the interrelated whole, Whitehead can agree with them that relations are the basis of "all philosophic thought," but with the proviso that they are "relations of number, and the relations of quantity, and of space" (*AE*, 86). Mathematicians had their own way of analyzing relations, as we shall see in the next chapter. Nevertheless the parts of an education are not inert units, as nuts and bolts of a machine. And no education can be judged as the sum of facts or pieces of information. The whole is dynamic and expressed as the development of power and style. "A merely well-informed man is the most useless bore on God's earth" (*AE*, 13). What he is advocating is that "mental cultivation" which is "the satisfactory way in which the mind will function when it is poked up into activity" (*AE*, 38).

Among the idealistic elements of Whitehead's philosophy are the stress on "an intimate sense for the power of ideas, the beauty of ideas, the structure of ideas—together with a particular body of knowledge which has peculiar reference to the life of the being possessing it" (*AE*, 23). Rarely has a thinker been more confident of the role of ideas in creating and destroying. ". . . Philosophy . . . is the most effective of all the intellectual pursuits. It builds cathedrals before the workmen have moved a stone, and it destroys them before the elements have worn down their arches. It is the architect of the buildings of the spirit, and it is also their solvent: —and the spiritual precedes the material" (*SMW*, x).

One of the important points is that ideas form a systematic whole. It may not be Hegel's Idea in history, but it is not any job lot of impressions and notions. Neither as education nor as philosophy are ideas a mere sum of items. In both there must be synthesis.

Just as an education is no mere arithmetical total of discrete pieces of information, such as the score on a number of true-false or multiple-choice questions, so a philosophy must necessarily be a synthesis. Whitehead the mathematician gives an account of synthesis that rests upon order.

Consider a group of things, concrete or abstract, material things or merely ideas of relations between other things. Let the individuals be denoted by letters *a, b . . . z*. Let any two of the group of things be capable of a synthesis which results in some third thing.

Let this synthesis be of such a nature that all the properties which are attributed to any one of the original group of things can be attributed to the result of this synthesis. Accordingly the resultant thing belongs to the original group.

Let the idea of order between the two things be attributable to their synthesis.

[It follows from this conception of which constituent comes first, that] $a \cap b$ and $b \cap a$ symbolize two different things.[7]

In mere addition, the order of items summed makes no difference, for $1 + 2 = 2 + 1$. The ordering makes which comes first a differentiating character of synthesis. Many familiar examples of the latter can be known from procedures of cooking.

There is necessarily a dialectic overcoming of antitheses or unresolved dualisms. There is so rich an array of examples that we must choose a few and suggest that the reader search out many more. This one seems to transfer the idea of the Absolute to each person: "A mind . . . should be both more abstract and more concrete" (*AE*, 24). This is a paradox unless we reflect that by abstract thought we gain generalizations. The more general an idea, the more things to which it can refer. If reality is essentially relational, then the idea that is most general refers to the most facts as they are together in a systematic whole. Clearly Whitehead is encouraging "that eye for the whole chessboard, for the bearing of one set of ideas on another" (*AE*, 24).

The mind that is both abstract and concrete is the mind of modern science, taking account both of "general principles" and of "irreducible and stubborn facts" (William James's description of his method, quoted *SMW*, 4). Whitehead always includes a strong emotional drive in the formation of temperament. "It is this union of passionate interest in the detailed facts with equal devotion to abstract generalization which forms the novelty of our present society. Previously it had appeared sporadically and as if by chance. This balance of mind has now become part of the tradition which infects cultivated thought. It is the salt which keeps life sweet. The main business of universities is to transmit this tradition as a widespread inheritance from generation to generation" (*SMW*, 4).

Among the dichotomies Whitehead overcomes is that between facts and values, typical of the application of the objective-subjective dualism. Because the apprehension of fact is aesthetic, quickened by art to a "vivid apprehension of value," the scientific mind need not consider itself indifferent to value, nor is the world, so apprehended, meaningless. In typical idealistic fashion, Whitehead takes all human institutions as illustration of one truth of our knowledge of reality. "Science, art, religion, morality, take their rise from this sense of values within the structure of being. Each individual embodies an adventure of existence. The art of life is the guidance of this adventure" (*AE*, 50).

The early educational essays show Whitehead groping to state his philosophy as a religious philosophy. In harmony with post-Kantian philosophers he stresses the moral essence of religion. He would inculcate "duty and reverence. Duty arises from our potential control over the course of events. Where attainable knowledge could have changed the issue; ignorance has the guilt of vice. And the foundation of reverence is this perception, that the present holds within itself the complete sum of existence, backwards and forwards, that whole amplitude of time, which is eternity" (*AE*, 26). In another passage he makes clearer that this moral essence is not moralism. "The great religions of civilization include . . . revolts against the inculcation of morals as a set of isolated prohibitions. Morality, in the petty negative sense of the term, is the deadly enemy of religion. . . . Every outbreak of religion exhibits the same intensity of antagonism" (*AE*, 50, appealing to Gospel denunciation of Pharisees and Paul's diatribe against the Law).

Such a religious philosophy, in keeping with nineteenth-century idealism, rejects all attempts to formulate religious truth in creeds, and quite coherently thinks of intense religion as the achievement of union with the divine. These are clear, again from "Freedom and Discipline." "Whatever be the right way to formulate religious truths, it is death to religion to insist on a premature stage of precision" (*AE*, 50). Religion, so conceived, is "the sense of value, the sense of importance. It takes the various forms of wonder, of curiosity, of reverence, of worship, of tumultuous desire for merging personality in something beyond itself" (*AE,* 51). But before 1925 there is nothing about God.

Whitehead's idealistic reconciliation of opposites can very often be found at the end of his essays. These conclusions have been tolerated as good rhetoric, a fitting way to bring the address to a climactic pitch. But they are more than that. They are the inevitable outcome of a dialectical synthesis. "The Organization of Thought" raises logic from the instrumental to the consumatory level:

Neither logic without observation, nor observation without logic, can move one step in the formation of science. We may conceive humanity as engaged in an internecine conflict between youth and age. Youth is not defined by years but by the creative impulse to make something. The aged are those who, before all things, desire not to make a mistake. Logic is the olive branch from the old to the young, the wand which in the hands of youth has the magic property of creating science. (*AE,* 122–23)

Only if logic has the purpose of critical restraint and of creative passion can it be synthetic and unifying.

One of Whitehead's applications of reconciliation is to the great social and political antithesis called "liberal" and "conservative." Whitehead's philosophy is in principle a middle course between individualism and collectivism, and the avoidance of the extremes of anarchy and dictatorship. It would not be expected in the third lecture of *Symbolism,* except that these were lectures at the University of Virginia, and Whitehead had great admiration for the type of Thomas Jefferson, "the liberal aristocrat" (*AE,* 56). Codes, rules of behavior, canons of art, are attempts to impose system which on the whole will promote favorable symbolic interconnections. As a community changes, all such rules and canons require revision in the light of reason. The object to be obtained has two aspects; one is the subordination of the community to the individuals composing it, and the other is the subordination of the individuals to the community.[8]

Conclusion

In the quest for order Whitehead both trusts logic to provide a definition and distrusts logic, for in experience we confront other types of definite relationships. What is definite in experience may or may not be defined in a logic of relations. The vaguely defined "rhythm," which is important in life and enjoyment, thus can maintain a respected place side by side with "series," which is "a relation that is asymmetrical, transitive, and connected." The latter is intellectually clear, as we shall see in the next chapter. Yet experience, which includes feeling and emotion, makes us acquainted not only with rhythms but with balance, hierarchy, and harmony. To divulge gradually how Whitehead's work had to take account of them prepares us in the end for a synthetic system. This we must anticipate also by considering our place in history, in which we must ask in what respects we have advanced beyond our fathers and mothers and in what respects our children may advance beyond us. Progress is one of many ways by which we order our history.

Several crucial questions are pertinent to following Whitehead in his quest for order. To begin: How many distinguishable kinds of order do we need to acknowledge? If we do distinguish the order of nature and the moral order, how are they related? Do we find the same modes of order in nature and in moral life, such as harmony, balance, hierarchy? Last, do these modes of order belong together in ways that show them to support or to inhibit one another?

Chapter Two

The Adventure of a Pythagorean Mind: The Logic of Order

A Pythagorean Vision

Whitehead concludes his chapter "Mathematics as an Element in the History of Thought" with a statement and a question: "Truly, Pythagoras in founding European philosophy and European mathematics, endowed them with the luckiest of lucky guesses—or, was it a flash of divine genius, penetrating to the inmost nature of things?" (*SMW*, 56). The problem of the discovery of numbers, relations, proportions, and order generally is that we are talking about aspects of things and connections between them that are "extremely unobvious" and "very remote from any notions which can be immediately derived by perception through the senses; unless indeed it be perception stimulated and guided by antecedent mathematical knowledge" (*SMW*, 29). So original is mathematics that it resembles music. Therefore it is said that we "divine . . . mathematical ideas which were waiting for discovery" (*SMW*, 30). Is there an ideal realm that is disclosed to insight that resembles the revelation to a prophet? Revelation is not unplausible although such insight is rare and unpredictable. Probably Whitehead is evoking our wonder and admiration rather than pressing an explanation. Meditating on positive and negative numbers, Whitehead concludes: "Surely it was from the clouds that the Germans fetched + and −; the ideas which these symbols have generated are much too important for the welfare of humanity to have come from the sea or from the land" (*IM*, 60).

Since mathematics is "the science of order," we need to know what the relation is to the regularities of nature. One account given by Whitehead of the origin of mathematics is on the basis of analysis rather than revelation. "The habit of such analysis enlightens every act of the functioning of the human mind. It first . . . emphasizes the direct aesthetic appreciation of the content of experience. . . . There is then the abstraction of the particular entities involved, viewed in themselves. . . . Lastly there is the further apprehension of the absolutely general conditions satisfied by the particular relations of those entities . . ." (*SMW*, 37). This is the pattern of romance, precision, and generalization.

Whether mathematics begins with revelation or with analysis, the subject in Western history began with Pythagoras, who invented the name "philosopher" because by tradition he claimed only to love wisdom rather than to be wise. Plato absorbed much of Pythagoras and transmitted a vision to us. Exactly which statement in Plato? We are referred to *The Sophist.* The Stranger presents the world as many things: "colors and forms and sores and vices and virtues . . . and countless others. . . ."[1] Of any actual existent, we say that it is a red cube, or a great sphere, or a good man. Hence the world may be conceived as an "intermingling," according as one characteristic participates in another. Now there are three possible states of affairs: "either all things will mingle with one another, or none will do so, or some will and others will not." As to nothing mingling with anything else, do we find a color, say red, that has no shape and size, or a shape that has no color? No. As to everything mingling with everything, do we find round squares or spherical cubes? No. Therefore we must deny that nothing participates with anything else, or that everything participates with anything else. We must affirm, since only these three are possible, that some things will participate and some things will not. Just as grammar shows us which words fit with which other words, so this "greatest of sciences."

Whitehead does not claim in his *Universal Algebra* or in *Principia Mathematica* (with Bertrand Russell) to have established this great science of "logical structures and of structures of structures," but he does convey to us the possibility that Plato's vision may transform man's knowledge of orders of all sorts, and be the greatest hope of our future. Whitehead never tires of telling us that between a prophet and the fulfillment of prophecy there may be three thousand, two thousand, one thousand years. He sees a parallel in history between the first fragmentary success of Pythagoras and such detailed knowledge of sound as was achieved in nineteenth-century physics. If this new science of *Principia Mathematica* seems now not to be effecting changes beyond esoteric circles of mathematicians, recall that "its applications may lie in a future as remote from today as were the modern applications in the lifetime of Pythagoras . . ." (*ESP*, 238).

We have suggested that Whitehead was a modern Pythagorean and that in quest of a vision his writings can be understood. That Pythagoras was a mere mathematician might have been inadvertently conveyed to us by a geometry book that told us of him only in connection with a theorem. Although a legendary figure of pre-Socratic thought, we are probably safe in regarding him as a religious leader, and a man with a keen interest in the structure of society and the beauty of musical harmony. The Pythagorean way of life combined community discipline under precepts with the romance of a search for salvation, and the discipline of exact thought, to establish an explanation of the cosmos. The solid scientific contribution of the founder of the community was the discovery that there is a reason why some sounds are harmonious together. The unobvious fact is the proportion of the strings of a lyre or the length of the pipes. The law is that the simpler ratios, such as 1:2, which we call the octave, commingle easily, as Plato later said, whereas the more complex ratios produce cacophony. Pythagoras' doctrine, of course, is not fully satisfactory, but he had generalized to a theory that stated propositions both for vibrating strings and columns of air. He produced a very simple hypothesis to explain what we sense. Whitehead admires these aspects of science; but above all, what is admirable is the courage to generalize from a bit of geometry and a bit of physics to the entire universe. The world is a cosmos, a world order, and the secret of its beauty and intelligibility lies in number. "All things are number," he said in his most daring moment—at least so Aristotle's story goes.[2]

We have begun a chapter on adventure by telling of two ancient intellectual ancestors. One might expect of a son of Pythagoras and Plato that he would defend tradition and deplore change and innovation. Here is the paradox and mystery of Whitehead. He had an unshakable confidence in the beauty and intelligibility of a timeless order, yet he constantly defended the necessity of change and adaptation to a future whose very constitution can only be dimly discerned. "The art of progress is to preserve order amid change, and to preserve change amid order" (PR, 515). The remarkable characteristic of Whitehead's philosophy is to have combined the Hegelian dialectic, with which the last chapter was concerned, with the Pythagorean stress on harmony. The search is for a "full universe, disclosed by ["for" in text] every variety of experience, . . . a universe in which every detail enters into its proper relationship with the immediate occasion" (SMW, 38). Since both great philosophers stand in the same rationalist tradition, Whitehead can write of 2,400 years between Pythagoras and Hegel. ". . . The concept of the real world as exhibiting the evolution of an idea can be traced back to the train of thought set going by Pythagoras" (SMW, 42).

Pythagorean Faith in Harmony

Among all the chapters in Whitehead that concern order, the most important statement of a Pythagorean faith is Chapter 1 of *Science and the Modern World*. Although there are many such books written to explain the remarkable spurt of the sciences since 1600, none is so clear about a central metaphysical conviction. Pythagoras had called it *kosmos* and this is indeed the heart of the Greek view of the world.[3] But the Greeks were more speculative and less empirical (Whitehead says "too intellectual"), and the death of what Archimedes began required a new element supplied by the Hebrews. Their minds fastened on the particulars in history and referred every event to one transcendent agent. When rationality is coupled with faith in divine power, we have the only source of modern science. "It must come from the medieval insistence on the rationality of God, conceived as with the personal energy of Jehovah and with the rationality of a Greek philosopher" (*SMW*, 18).

Whitehead is trying to state an ultimate presupposition, a basic "mind set" or natural belief underlying what we do, and so deep that we do not need to formulate it or defend it. Therefore a careful reading of Whitehead's claim will require asking: am I committed to the discovery of order? It should also be accompanied by inquiry into what is assumed in our culture, particularly by scientists. It is also a most valuable guide to the reading of past and present philosophers.

"In the first place, there can be no living science unless there is a widespread instinctive conviction in the existence of an *Order of Things*, and, in particular, of an *Order of Nature*" (*SMW*, 5). Whitehead fails to distinguish these two orders here, but insists that the belief has become "instinctive." "It doesn't matter what men say in words, so long as their activities are controlled by settled instincts" (*SMW*, 5). This is reiterated later with an explanation. "Every detail was supervised and ordered: the search into nature could only result in the vindication of the faith in rationality" (*SMW*, 18).

But what does Whitehead do with the counterevidence of chance events for which there is no explanation? What of real randomness and accidents that cannot be predicted? Whitehead allows the contrast: "Men expected the sun to rise, but the wind bloweth where it listeth" (*SMW*, 7; John 3:8).[4] The context indicates that chance events are really exceptions to "the broad recurrences," and that acting on faith men enlarge the areas of predictability, reducing the number of events to which we do not yet know the explanation. But we must ask, is this faith in order committing us to identifying the real with the rational, and as Hegel added, the rational with the real? No, there is an ultimate to which there is no explanation. Even though we must finally accept the brute fact that there is a world rather than nothing, the strategy of Whitehead is to stick to explaining as long and far and deeply as possible, and to give up only at the end. There is irrationality, but only an ultimate irrationality.

By identifying the Western faith in order with the God of the Bible, has not Whitehead compromised philosophy, subjected reason to faith, as did some Medievals, and confused the kind of "god" of philosophy, as Aristotle's prime mover, with the Creator and Judge of the Judeo-Christian tradition who takes a part in guiding history, directing prophets and kings and priests, and subjecting mankind to judgment? How does Whitehead respond to this objection? The answer must wait until we examine what Whitehead means by "God" and how he frees the concept from many traditional associations and from any institutional supervision. This we shall do in Chapter 7 after the general categoreal scheme, Chapter 6.

Whitehead's statement of faith is at the conclusion of Chapter 1 of *Science and the Modern World*. We need to remember that Pythagoras was adopted by Jews, Christians, and Moslems of the Middle Ages as a prophet. He is extolled as a man of humility by St. Augustine in the *City of God* and he is the only philosopher mentioned in the saint's dialogues *Of Order*. Whitehead stands in this tradition, sometimes called Christian Platonism. He cites a sixteenth-century Italian heretic, Paolo Sarpi, who refused the notion of authoritarian control and dictated creed. "They asked," says Whitehead, "that *reason* should be used" (*SMW*, 27).

Faith in reason is the trust that the ultimate natures of things lie together in a harmony which excludes mere arbitrariness. It is the faith that at the base of things we shall not find mere arbitrary mystery. The faith in the order of nature which has made possible the growth of science is a particular example of a deeper faith. This faith cannot be justified by any inductive generalization. It springs from direct inspection of the nature of things disclosed in our own immediate present experience. . . . To experience this faith is to know that in being ourselves we are more than ourselves: to know that our experience, dim and fragmentary as it is, yet sounds the utmost depths of reality: to know that the detached details merely in order to be themselves demand that they should find themselves in a system of things: to know that this system includes the *harmony* of logical rationality, and the *harmony* of aesthetic achievement: to know that, while the *harmony* of logic lies upon the world as an iron necessity, the aesthetic *harmony* stands before it as a living ideal moulding the general flux in its broken progress towards finer, subtler issues. (*SMW*, 27–28, italics added)

The passage above shows a version of Pythagorean faith that over the centuries affirmed a fourfold harmony, of mathematics, of astronomy, of the soul, and of the society. In the "harmony of logical rationality" Whitehead links the mathematical and the physical. In the "aesthetic harmony" he links the soul and society. We have printed the passage with "harmony," emphasizing each of four occurrences. Although this passage shows Whitehead simplifying the harmonies, stating that the four are really basically two, we shall see later in studying the doctrine of harmony in *The Adventures of Ideas* that specifying the harmonies requires an expansion to a ninefold statement of faith.

"Order" Defined

We cannot now question that Whitehead has established the importance of order. Since he has used the rhythms and cycles of nature, we must grant that the husbandman cannot live unless he observes the seasons and the sailor must observe the tides. To know the sequences is to have a ground for prediction. We all have this familiarity, but the idea can be challenged as vague, even obscure, and importance is not a substitute for clarity.

Consider how all events are interconnected. When we see lightning, we listen for thunder; when we hear the wind, we look for the waves on the sea; in the chill autumn, the leaves fall. *Everywhere order reigns,* so that when some circumstances have been noted we can foresee that others will also be present. The progress of science consists in observing these interconnections and in sharing with a patient ingenuity that the events of this ever-shifting world are but examples of a few general connections or relations called laws. To see what is general in what is particular and what is permanent in what is transitory is the aim of scientific thought. (*IM*, 3–4, italics added)

Whitehead expresses fear that the mathematical concept of order might be considered trivial. It is indeed obvious that there are series of numbers in arithmetic and series of geometrical shapes, but these "are the simplest examples of an important general theory" (*IM*, 144). Whereas traditionally mathematics had been defined as "the science of number and quantity," or sometimes "the science of discrete and continuous magnitude," Whitehead redefines mathematics as "the science of order" (*ESP*, 195). Why is this so important?

One approach stresses the relevance of such a general science of order to all events whatsoever. We can now recognize that a science of order, more abstract than the usual branches of mathematics, would apply to more cases and therefore be more useful. Sometimes the subject is presented in full abstraction. Sometimes it is presented in specific cases. Whitehead does both, and only if we have the approaches together can we recognize the importance. Whitehead is quite willing to illustrate order, more specifically serial order, or series, from the sort of list that a people has of its chief executives. Had Whitehead written of order in America he might have appealed to presidents from Washington to Reagan (to bring the series to the present).

The general mathematical idea of a series is that of a set of things ranged in order, that is, in sequence. This meaning is accurately represented in the common use of the term. Consider, for example, the series of English Prime Ministers during the nineteenth century, arranged in the order of their first tenure of that office. . . . The series commences with William Pitt and ends with Lord Roseberry, who appropriately enough, is the biographer of the first member. (*IM*, 144)

Now Whitehead answers the objection that the subject is trivial: by analyzing ordering we discover the principle implicit in history books. What no historian mentions is that there are any number of other ways of arranging the same given facts.

We might have considered other serial orders for the arrangement of these men; for example, according to their height or their weight. These other suggested orders strike us as trivial in connection with Prime Ministers, and would not naturally occur to the mind; but abstractly they are just as good orders as any other. (ibid.)

This is no mere curiosity, for much of the mathematics Whitehead dealt with in *Universal Algebra,* 1897, and Russell dealt with in *Principles of Mathematics,* 1903, concerned series of numbers, continuous or discrete, finite or infinite.[5] Hitherto mathematicians had ignored many orderings and attended only to one important and obvious kind.

When one order among terms is very much more important or more obvious than other orders, it is often spoken of as *the* order of those terms. Thus *the* order of the integers would always be taken to mean their order as arranged in order of magnitude. But of course there is an indefinite number of other ways of arranging them. When the number of things considered is finite, the number of ways of arranging them in order is called the number of their permutations. (*IM*, 144–45)

Whitehead then goes on to show how the number of possible arrangements is not only "large" with relation to the number of things, but increases very quickly. "As *n* [the number of things] increases, the value of n! [the product of permutation] increases very quickly; thus 100! is a hundred times as large as 99!" (ibid.).

It was probably Russell who first classified relations as being (1) reflexive or irreflexive, (2) symmetrical or asymmetrical, (3) transitive or atransitive, (4) connected or unconnected, and who devised the simple symbolism and terminology that have become very widespread, almost universal, at the present time. Whitehead adopted the terminology and symbolism, which we illustrate, and helped to get it adopted.

We must first understand *what is meant by "order,"* that is by *"serial arrangement."* An order of a set of things is to be sought in that *relation holding between members of the set* which constitutes that order. The set viewed as a class has many orders. Thus the telegraph posts along a certain road have a space-order very obvious to our sense; but they have also a time-order according to dates of erection, perhaps more important to the postal authorities who replace them after fixed intervals. A set of cardinal numbers have an order of magnitude, often called the order of the set because of its insistent obviousness to us; but, if they are the numbers drawn in a lottery, their time order of occurrence in that drawing also ranged them in an order of some importance. (*ESP*, 197)

Order is defined by the "serial" relation. A relation (R) is serial when

(1) it implies diversity, so that, if *x* has the relation R to *y*, *x* is diverse from *y*;

(2) it is transitive, so that if *x* has the relation R to *y* and *y* to *z* then *x* has the relation R to *z*;

(3) it has the property of *connexity*, so that if *x* and *y* are things to which any things bear the relation R, or which bear the relation R to any things, then either *x* is identical with *y*, or *x* has the relation R to *y*, or *y* has the relation R to *x*.

These conditions are necessary and sufficient to secure that our ordinary ideas of "preceding" and "succeeding" hold in respect to the relation R. *The "field" of relation R is the class of things ranged in order by it* (*ESP*, 197–98).

A relation that ranges terms in order might just as well be defined as one that is asymmetrical, transitive, and connected. Then the factor of diversity or irreflexivity follows, just as above asymmetry (called "preceding" or "succeeding") follows from diversity, transitivity, and connexity. Both Whitehead and Russell also derive the notion of serial order from the relation "between."

Now it is not immediately obvious to everyone why order is elevated to so high a rank among the fundamental ideas of logic and mathematics. The reader who is not a professional need not take the authors' word for the centrality of order, trusting that the two independent books, *Universal Algebra* and *Principles of Mathematics,* together with the three volumes by the coauthors, *Principia Mathematica,* are correctly reasoned. For both Whitehead and Russell were popularizers of genius as well as original mathematicians. Already we have quoted from Whitehead's brilliant *Introduction to Mathematics,* originally published in 1911 in the *Home University Library.* Russell wrote his *Introduction to Mathematical Philosophy* in 1918, while in prison; it also has been many times reprinted. (The chapter "The Definition of Order" carries the subject a bit farther than possible here.) We have also quoted from the articles done separately and together by Whitehead and Russell for the great Eleventh Edition of the *Encyclopaedia Britannica* ("Mathematics," "Non-Euclidian Geometry," "Axioms of Geometry," republished in *Essays in Science and Philosophy,* 1948).[6] Whitehead is at his best in two papers, both easily available now, in which he shows the application of symbolic logic to the structure of scientific thought. The first paper was done before *Principia Mathematica* had been published, and is called "On Mathematical Concepts of the Material World" (published 1906).[7] The second was published after *P.M.*[8] and served as the title essay of *The Organization of Thought* and is now included in *The Aims of Education.* The reader may well begin his study of logic with the latter; we shall shortly explain why.

An Order of Things

What could Whitehead have meant by faith in an "Order of Things"? Earlier we saw this contrasted to an "Order of Nature." What contrast is this in our experience? The best passage from which we can begin to recognize the forms of definiteness that can be abstracted from concrete actualities comes from *Modes of Thought*:

The most simple doctrine about types of being is that some extreme type exists independently of the rest of things. For example, Greek philosophers, and in particular Plato, seem to have held this doctrine in respect to qualitative abstractions, [quantitative abstractions] such as number, [and] geometrical relations, moral characteristics, and the qualitative disclosures of the higher sense-perceptions. . . . According to this tradition insofar as we abstract from our experience the brute particularity of happening here, and now, amid this environment, there remains a residue with self-identities, differences and essential interconnections, which seem to have no essential reference to the passage of events. According to this doctrine, as the result of this discard of the factor of transition we rivet our attention on the eternal realm of forms. In this imagined realm there is no passage, no loss, no gain. It is complete in itself. It is self-sustaining. It is therefore the realm of the "completely real."

. . . We must admit that in some sense or other, we inevitably presuppose this realm of forms, in abstraction from passage, loss, and gain. For example, the multiplication table up to "twelve-times-twelve" is a humble member of it. In all our thought of what has happened and can happen, we presuppose the multiplication table as essentially qualifying the course of history, whenever it is relevant. It is always at hand, and there is no escape.[9]

This passage is illuminating because although 144 is nothing actual in itself, it nevertheless is not only 12×12, it is also 6×24, and also 3×48, and also ½ of 288, etc. If "order" means for one thing to have a fixed relationship to other things, whatever these numbers are, they are orderly, and indeed more orderly than the concrete things we experience. Although abstract, they are not vague or elusive; they also are "certain knowledge." Indeed, they are more clear than, say, loaves of bread. We may make a mistake in counting the loaves to 144, and group them by dozens to keep track of their quantity. But do we not check our accuracy in counting against the model calculation of the system? This may be all very convincing; but if the multiplication table is but a "humble member" of the Order of Things, what might be some member of greater status than quantity?

Although numbers are a common example, there are also colors. Just as Whitehead often meditated on what twoness is, so he often asked, what is whiteness? Not anything concretely real because as such it is not anywhere or at any time, yet something we encounter in experiencing concrete realities. Whitehead contrasts the concrete reality of a mountain to a color. "The mountain endures. But when after ages it has been worn away, it has gone. . . . A color is eternal. It haunts time like a spirit. It comes and it goes. But where it comes it is the same color. It neither survives nor does it live. It appears when it is wanted" (*SMW,* 126). This is the passage in which he explains why these forms are called "eternal objects." This is puzzling because "object" means nothing like a physical object or commonsense "thing" like a chair. It is rather an "object of thought," and is compared to "idea" in other philosophies. Although there is a religious connotation to "eternal," this is a reflection of Plato's conception of the Heaven of Forms.

Now we might object that although quantity is objectively real, there somehow in nature as is a fixed proportion of hydrogen to oxygen in water, perhaps the color of a thing observed is only our response to wavelengths of light particles. When Whitehead calls a color "eternal," a something that "haunts time like a spirit," does this not become excessively metaphysical in the sense of going beyond what we can know? Are we postulating ghosts? Whitehead seems to concede that his universe is haunted, and we might then conclude that he is propagating superstition. Yet regarded as what is common between all experienced patches of a given color, this is a standard which we not only have in mind by which to judge, but an experience in which we say, "this resembles that so closely that we see no difference between them." If it is meaningful to say that *a* and *b* are of the same or identical color, then that identical color has a status transcending this and that. This standard white, called "whiteness," would in some systems even be given the dignity of being "white." Some philosophers follow Plato more closely, and say that the "white" is more real and better than any example of white things. Whitehead does not say that "White" is whiter than white, or more real than white things, but only that it belongs to a different order or realm that is not in time or in space. Consider among colors their arrangement according to the dimensions, calling them hue, brightness, and intensity. Among hues, contrast yellow to orange to red to violet to blue to green. Make each patch the most intense. Is there not a relationship of closeness to or distance from the purest white? Here is a structural order of color theory, one to which every child gains access by color wheels constructed by mixing pigments. The question is, as with the multiplication table, about an order other than that of agencies that have locus in space and time. Whitehead does not spell out his argument, but we can see that his appeal is the very opposite of superstition; it is to theory.

Although Whitehead cannot claim that "eternal objects" do anything, he does argue that without definiteness there cannot be the events of nature. Since he includes not only colors and "geometrical characteristics" (which we used above as a red sphere), which can, in Plato's example, "mingle," there are also sounds and scents. There are "things" meaning things which we can sense and think of and talk about and embody. They are other than nature and are said to transcend events, "the ultimate units[s] of natural occurrence." As in traditional theories of universals, they can be shared by particular events. "This interfusion of events is effected by the aspects of those eternal objects . . . which are required for nature and are not emergent from it" (*SMW*, 151).

When Whitehead refers to eternal objects as constituting a "realm," what more could he mean? The clearest answer is that of our red sphere; it is possible that it could have been blue, or possible that it could have been a cube. There are innumerable alternative colors and shapes. Is it meaningful to say of the red sphere that it is blue, or to say of it that it is a cube? By having a realm of alternative colors and shapes, such propositions can be meaningful, however false they are. This is no mere puzzle of language. "The real relevance of untrue propositions for each actual occasion is disclosed by art, romance, and by criticism in reference to ideals. It is the foundation of the metaphysical position . . . the understanding of actuality requires a reference to ideality. The two realms are intrisically inherent in the total metaphysical situation. The truth that some proposition respecting an actual occasion is untrue may express the vital truth as to the aesthetic achievement" (*SMW*, 228).

The above passage needs to be studied in the light of logic. Whitehead is considering what is possible and impossible or what can and cannot be together. Is it false that a real three-dimensional object, one with weight and size and mass, of some material, and whatever else we may specify as marks of "the physical," can be at the same time both a sphere and a cube? Consider the meanings. A sphere has one surface. A cube has six plane surfaces. Obviously we should answer that a solid object cannot have both one and six surfaces. We should call it contradictory for anyone to claim such an object. It would be absurd even to look for such a thing. But we may be confronted with the question, were not the ancient Pythagoreans more clever than we? Maybe they made such things which seem impossible to us, but perhaps the followers lost the formula and the trick of overcoming logic. Maybe more clever generations will devise techniques! If we reject these as impossible, and do not need to consult history or peer prophetically into the future, then we are claiming access to a realm or an order which is a paragon of logic. Some philosophers used to call it the "Intelligible World," and Whitehead can be read as a revision of the tradition. But now the question must give us pause. Is there not only this one concrete world? Who wants to be "otherworldly"? Is that not even worse than believing in ghosts, something like turning one's gaze to a heaven of forms, as though we could be like angels contemplating their beauty? Is not Whitehead deceiving himself, if he is honest, and even worse, trying to deceive us? What is the basis in experience? And what is the relation between these orders or realms?

Although there is a definite relationship between spheres and cubes, made clear in geometry, and a definite relationship between red and blue, made clear in color theory, etc., each of these "eternal objects" is exactly what it is. Whitehead calls them "essences," probably because when he was writing there were philosophers who claimed that these were what could be known directly, or by acquaintance. It is not uncommon to say that we must "abstract" them, that is, take them apart from relationship to the natural events. Consequently Whitehead does not mean that eternal objects can be fully real by themselves (*SMW*, 228–29). Moreover, "an eternal object, considered as an abstract entity, cannot be divorced from its reference to other eternal objects" (*SMW*, 229–30). This Whitehead calls having a "relational essence" (*SMW*, 230). These essences as a whole are related to each actuality, but since they are infinite in number and it is finite, very few need ordinarily be considered.

Whitehead is then not turning us away from white things to White or whiteness, as though these eternal objects are better than the actualities that are white. And we are acquainted with them in our experience of the fully real world. Since we abstract them to consider them as such, they are only aspects of real things. So it is misleading to capitalize "Things" as though they had a status of greater dignity—as Plato said of the Ideas, "really real." It might then be better to say that these are the structures that make it possible for things to be and to be intelligible to us. With these interpretations, we might concede that they are important in answering the question, how can we know natural things? We do claim to know kinds of things as well as members of these classes. Although Whitehead disclaims identifying universals with classes, we can see that his account would allow some universals to be class kinds. The traditional illustration of a universal was horseness as contrasted to particular horses. Perhaps it is better to anticipate the next chapter by saying that Whitehead is concerned with how there can be a nature which we characterize as lawful. If a law covers unobserved cases and even unobservable cases, as of a future, ever not yet actual, how is this possible? If we find structures essential to real things that have the relations described as arithmetical, geometrical, qualitative, and logical, then there is only the difficulty of spelling out how these are the possibilites which as actualized show us what is likely and give us a basis for judging what is impossible and what is necessary.

We have seen that the importance of an alternative to what a thing is allows meaningful false propositions, as well as criticism and the idealizing tendencies of art and romance. The "status of an eternal object is that of a possibility for an actuality. Every actual occasion is defined as to its character by how these possibilities are actualised for that occasion. Thus actualisation is a selection among possibilities" (*SMW*, 229). Several passages indicate that only if we accord an important status to the eternal objects can there be meaningful change in process. It is certainly true that a reality that includes possibility also includes the possibility of changing into something better. We need eternal objects to have definite knowledge of actuality, but even more we need this realm for hope that something better can be actualized. It follows, as Whitehead argues, that eternal objects are not solely of importance for theory of knowledge.

The chapter "Abstraction" in *Science and the Modern World* is followed immediately by the chapter "God." In this he gives an account of the envisagement of the realm of eternal objects, and perhaps its order comes from being graded in vision, as well as from relevance to actualities. Whitehead needs a realm of eternal objects to account for religion, defined as "the reaction of human nature to its search for God" (*SMW*, 274).

Religion is the vision of something which stands beyond, behind, and within, the passing flux of immediate things; something which is real, and yet waiting to be realized; something which is a remote possibility, and yet the greatest of present facts; something that gives meaning to all that passes, and yet eludes apprehension; something whose possession is the final good, and yet is beyond all reach; something which is the ultimate ideal and the hopeless quest. (*SMW*, 275).

We have not yet seen how Whitehead's philosophy is one that requires God. Perhaps the best way to make sense of this theistic metaphysics is to say that the forms themselves are not acts. There is no other world, as a heaven that is as real or even more real than this world. These essences as the ground of our hope, and the explanation of change for the better, can be understood only as part of God's vision. Exactly how God, a cosmic mind, envisions them, is of course beyond our knowing. Yet in experience we know the aim toward ideals. We must ourselves begin with vision in order to comprehend the beauty, adventure, and peace of the process.

One clearly intelligible ordering of eternal objects is hierarchical. That there is a gradation is clear specifically because they range from simple to complex. "An eternal object, such as a definite shade of green, which cannot be analyzed into a relationship of components, will be called 'simple.' This is the grade of zero complexity" (*SMW*, 240). Then any number of simple components together, called *A, B, C*, can be a relationship. "To take a simple example, *A, B, C* may be three definite colors with the spatio-temporal relatedness to each other of the three faces of a regular tetrahedron, anywhere at any time. The *R (A, B, C)* is another eternal object of the lowest complex grade. Analogously there are eternal objects of successively higher grades" (ibid.). This is only an example of one "abstractive hierarchy," with a base in colors, and presumably other eternal objects, among which Whitehead sometimes cites emotions, which could be so analyzed, but this is left to the reader to carry out.

Is a hierarchy finite or infinite? Presumably, if the realm includes innumerable simple eternal objects, the number of combinations could never be exhausted. Yet some are said to be finite. By this Whitehead means to "possess a grade of maximum complexity." This highest grade cannot be a component of any higher complex, and necessarily "this grade of maximum complexity must possess only one member . . ." (*SMW*, 243). We may begin with this "vertex" and work our way down, level by level, to simple eternal objects. In working out his theory Whitehead talks of the bottom and top of the hierarchy, but unlike medieval schemes, his does not fill out the intermediary levels with an exact count, three, five, seven, nine. Apparently this struck Whitehead as going beyond the evidence.

"Any actual occasion α [has] a group g of simple eternal objects which are ingredient in that group in the most concrete mode. This complete ingredience in an occasion, so as to yield the most complete fusion of individual essence with other eternal objects in the formation of the individual emergent occasion, is evidently of its own kind and cannot be defined in terms of anything else" (*SMW*, 244). Since no description of all the eternal objects associated with α can be complete, this hierarchy is infinite (*SMW*, 245). Although generally we abstract from possibilities, and begin, as we have done, with simples, these are actually the last things we arrive at when we begin from actual occasions. These two forms of abstraction "run in the opposite direction . . ." (*SMW*, 245). This may explain some of the difficulties we encounter in understanding abstraction and eternal objects. Rather than doing the subject in a logical or mathematical way, we could begin from an experience, for its own sake, of an actual occasion as "an aesthetic synthesis." Then we would deal with "the shape, or pattern, or form, of the occasion. . . ." Since Whitehead does deal with the actual occasions of the highest complexity, the institutions studied historically, religions, civilization, modern science, etc., we need in later chapters to remember that whatever we can say about them can only suggest the infinite and inexhaustible, eternal objects that together are the "shape, or pattern, or form, of the occasion insofar as the occasion is constituted of what enters into its full realization" (*SMW*, 245).

Some readers are helped in thinking of the forms to find Whitehead refer to proportions of oxygen to carbon. In isolating the abstracted elements chemistry has been a distinct success. We all know different formulas for carbon monoxide and carbon dioxide (*MT*, 193–95). This example, which recurs in Whitehead's writings, is an appeal to the success of chemistry.[10]

Whitehead has other ways of expressing the reliance of science on a double order. One way that carries us beyond is the dipolar conception of the process of becoming: "Fact and Form" (*PR*, 62–94). With a shift toward the contrast between observation and conception we find also the thesis that "coordinated knowledge . . . is formed by the meeting of two orders of experience" (*AI*, 198).

Conclusion

The scope of a Pythagorean mind has often been admired. If reason is given numbers, and reflects upon a world in which numbers are one clue to its intelligibility, what follows? Nothing short of a vision such as Plato's including forms and God. Although the technical conclusion about these eternal objects or essences, that they are merely possible, not actual, yet real as potential for actualization, is closer to Aristotle, yet the inspiration is Plato's; and the results are more Platonic than Aristotelian.

We have not exhausted the theme of Whitehead's Pythagorean vision, particularly the way the eternal objects are ordered. Since there is "mutual immanence," we have regarded the Order of Nature as subject to the logical order of the Order of Things. There is also a way in which "the process of finite history is essential for the ordering of the basic vision. . . ."

Perhaps the more important modification of Plato's vision is not so much the Aristotelian modification as the Hegelian.

The notion of the one perfection of order, which is (I believe) Plato's doctrine, must go the way of the one possible geometry. The universe is more various, more Hegelian. (*ESP*, 90)

Does Whitehead mean to introduce a plurality into the Order of Things, such that we can give an account of a succession of orders? We have worked with the notion of one interconnected realm of eternal objects, but perhaps what we now need is a two-tier system of higher-level possibilities, which are properly eternal or timeless, and a lower tier of possibilities in which only the realization of one set of possibilities makes possible another successor set of possibilities. This would be the introduction of process into eternity, which does indeed sound contradictory until one reflects upon the levels. If the following passage is only cosmology, then it is only that the Order of Nature illustrates a succession of types. But if this Order of Nature is also reciprocally immanent in the Order of Things, then there must be a corresponding succession of realms of possibles. But is it conceivable that there are old and tired possibilities and new and fresh possibilities? Our Platonic tradition would lead us to discount this succession as contradictory. Our Hegelian tradition would incline us to admit the following vision as more coherent:

Enlarge your view of the final fact which is permanent amid change. In its essence, realization is limitation, exclusion. But this ultimate fact includes in its appetitive vision all possibilities of order, possibilities at once incompatible and unlimited with a fecundity beyond imagination. Finite transcience stages this welter of incompatibles in their ordered relevance to the flux of epochs. . . . (*ESP*, 89)

Chapter Three

The Order of Experience: From Nature Dead to Nature Alive—Part One

Experience: Bringing Order Out of Disorder

If beginning with the logic of order has suggested that we begin with order in experience, then, argues Whitehead, we have been most seriously deceived. In reality we begin with *tohu va bohu* or chaos or a mess and try to reach the intelligible and the meaningful. Actual experience is of a

flux of perceptions, sensations, and emotions. . . . The most obvious aspect of this field of actual experience is its disorderly character. It is for each person a *continuum*, fragmentary, and with elements not clearly differentiated. The comparison of the sensible experiences of diverse people brings its own difficulties. I insist on the radically untidy, ill-adjusted character of the fields of actual experience. . . . (*AE*, 109)

The epistemological problem of order is not at all like the logical problem of order. That is, in "The Organization of Thought," it is not at all how to define the necessary and sufficient conditions of a serial or other formal type of order. It is an attempt to explain how we come to isolate and relate such an object as a chair. Out of the flux of impressions we become aware of what we believe is the same object, in spite of different circumstances, times, and projects. Whitehead stresses what we achieve conceptually in the commonsense idea of "that chair." Thereby we interrelate

the experience of the folk who made it, of the folk who sold it, of the folk who have seen and used it, of the man who is now experiencing a comfortable sense of support, combined with our expectations of an analogous future, terminated finally by a different set of experiences when the chair collapses and becomes firewood. The formation of that type of concept was a tremendous job. . . . (*AE,* 110)

We must state the problem because we must explore the detailed answer. Although we encounter disorder, we get to the orderly nature presented in scientific theory: "exact instants of time, in a space formed by exact points, without parts and without magnitude: the neat, trim, tidy, exact world which is the goal of scientific thought" (*AE,* 109).

Not only common sense but mathematics (arithmetic, algebra, general-function theory, analysis) is necessary to achieve order out of disorder, and a necessary metaphysical aspect is faith in an order of nature.

Although Whitehead appeals to a shared or common faith in "an Order of Nature," he is not content to let the matter remain implicit or on the level of instinct. It is not sufficient to say "of course we all share in this faith" because there are explicit philosophies that "deny the rationality of science. This conclusion lies upon the surface of Hume's philosophy" (*SMW,* 5). Whitehead considers Hume's doctrine of contiguity and succession of atomic bits. They reveal no causation we could know from the nature of either cause or effect. This doctrine reveals much of the subjective bias of modern philosophy and also is the implicit philosophy of much of modern science.[1] Later we shall see that the discoveries of subatomic physics forced the scientific thought of our century to admit exceptions to the continuity of movement spatially and temporally (below, at end of next section). Whitehead grants that however inadequate Hume's philosophy, scientists need not be metaphysicians to make successful discoveries. Indeed, metaphysics may distract a scientist from his specific theory and from specific data. Yet there is a lurking danger that modern science is running on an inherited faith "to remove . . . the philosophic mountain" (*SMW,* 6). Had *Science and the Modern World* been written twenty or forty years later, Whitehead could have cited all those doctrines of the absurd to which any doctrine of the rationality of events is foreign and that anathematize any "conviction in the existence of an *Order of Things* and, in particular, of an *Order of Nature*" (*SMW,* 5). Yet Whitehead opposed in principle what positivism stated and existentialism dramatized.

It may well be that Whitehead had struggled through an attempt to state the order of nature in a Kantian way as product of our categories. The context of "Space, Time, and Relativity" indicates that he accepted to some extent Kant's doctrine that mind begins "from . . . *disjecta membra* as its sole datum. It is not true that we are directly aware of a smooth running world, which in our speculations we are to conceive as given. In my view the creation of the world is the first unconscious act of speculative thought, and the first task of a self-conscious philosophy is to explain how it has been done" (*AE*, 165).

Although Whitehead may once have accepted the notion of the "physical world" as a "deduced concept" or some sort of postulated or constructed object, in his completed philosophy he explicitly rejected Kant's theory of order.[2]

The philosophy of organism is the inversion of Kant's philosophy. *The Critique of Pure Reason* describes the process by which subjective data pass into the appearance of an objective world. The philosophy of organism seeks to describe how objective data pass into subjective satisfaction, and how order in the objective data provides intensity in the subjective satisfaction. For Kant, the world emerges from the subject; for the philosophy of organism, the subject emerges from the world—a "superject" rather than a "subject." . . . The degree of order in the datum is measured by the degree of richness in the objective lure. (*PR*, 135–36)

The theories of order rejected by Whitehead are not only Hume's and Kant's but any theory that the order of nature is merely our observation or a mind-imposed regularity. Whitehead rejects not only Hume and Kant but Hegel also: "For such schemes, ordered experience is the result of schematization of modes of *thought*, concerning causation, substance, quality, quantity" (*PR*, 172). Any such simple theory of order as mere physical regularity is also too simple (*SMW*, 25–26). The logic of Whitehead's position is that the order of nature is a complex matter. There are many grounds or principles, not only one.

We are left then with two theories of order that can be taken seriously. Order or law of nature may be either imposed or immanent. Sometimes Whitehead indicates that he is contrasting Semitic monotheism of the Bible to Plato's immanentist view of the *Timaeus*. Other times he uses the Moslem view of Allah on one side and the Buddhist view of Dharma on the other (*AI*, 154, 173).[3]

Although religiously Whitehead is offended by the doctrine of omnipotence, and rarely treats it other than to make a polemical attack upon it, he seems genuinely impressed by the merits of the theory that law has been imposed upon events. It was historically necessary that men ignore the apparent capriciousness of events and affirm unobvious regularities. Only thus could science have developed, and this faith was essential to the great success of science (*AI,* 146). Second, the sturdy realism of the doctrine is its strength. Says Whitehead, paying respects to Newton:

> . . . the Laws of Nature will be exactly obeyed. Certainly, what God meant he did. When He said, Let there be light, there was *light* and not mere imitation or a statistical average. Thus the statistical notion, though it may explain some facts of our confused perception, is not applicable to the ultimate, imposed laws. (*AI,* 145)

Third, the imposition theory does not evade the question, what shall we expect in the future? " . . . Apart from some notion of imposed Law, the doctrine of immanence provides absolutely no reason why the universe should not be steadily relapsing into lawless chaos" (*AI,* 146–47).

Yet Whitehead, taking the immanentist side of the dialogue, presents a stronger case for this alternative. Since we do not discover exact repetition of patterns, "the exact conformation of nature to any law is not to be expected" (*AI,* 143). The immanentist alternative does not require us to oversimplify. The laws we know are those of our epoch only:

> since the laws of nature depend on the individual characters of the things constituting nature, as the things change, then correspondingly the laws will change. Thus the modern evolutionary view of the physical universe should conceive of the laws of nature as evolving concurrently with the things constituting the environment. Thus the conception of the Universe as evolving subject to fixed, eternal laws regulating all behavior should be abandoned. (*AI,* 143)

Further, with regard to the methods of empirical science:

> a reason [is] now . . . produced why we should put some limited trust in induction. For if we assume an environment largely composed of a sort of existences whose nature we partly understand, then we have some knowledge of the laws of nature dominating that environment. (*AI,* 143)

Whitehead adduces other reasons but the strongest that counts for immanentism against impositionism is the latter, quoted at length. The transcendental view, although it guarantees that the future will be exactly like the past, fails to account for the emergence of new order. The evolution of new species is one illustration of the epochal view of orders in succession (cf. *AI,* 143–73).

Whitehead's struggle toward an adequate theory of order in metaphysics is to escape between the horns of materialism and traditional theism. He writes in the section "The Order of Nature":

Until the last few years the sole alternatives were: either the material universe, with its present type of order, is eternal; or else it came into being, and will pass out of being, according to the fiat of Jehovah. Thus, on all sides, Plato's allegory of the evolution of a new type of order based on new types of dominant societies became a daydream, puzzling to commentators. (*PR,* 146)

Whitehead's last word on the dialogue between an immanentist and an impositionist seems to be a reconciliation or a synthesis. I say "seems" because Whitehead does this through citing Clement of Alexandria. How does "the primordial Being, who is the source of the inevitable recurrence of the world towards order, share . . . his nature with the world?"

In some sense he is a component in the natures of all fugitive things. Thus, an understanding of the nature of temporal things involves a comprehension of the immanence of the Eternal Being. This doctrine effects an important reconciliation between the doctrines of Imposed Law and Immanent Law. . . . The necessity of the trend towards order does not arise from the imposed will of a transcendent God. It arises from the fact that the existents in nature are sharing in the nature of the immanent God. (*AI,* 166)

Nature Is Cosmos

If one surveys Whitehead's conceptions of an order of nature, one must begin with "On Mathematical Concepts of the Material World." This is an application of symbolic logic before the publication of *Principia Mathematica,* but much of the philosophy can be understood without the symbols. We confront "many possible ways of conceiving the nature of the material world." The problem is limited, and therefore defined, as that of the relations of

the ultimate entities which (in ordinary language) constitute the "stuff" in space. An abstract logical statement of this limited problem . . . is as follows: Given a set of entities which form the field of a certain polyadic (i.e., many-termed) relation R, what "axioms" satisfied by R have as their consequence that the theorems of Euclidian geometry are the expressions of certain properties of the field of R?[4]

As a geometer Whitehead is concerned with the basis of the conception of points of space, and it is of interest to note that motion and time are added to the scheme of stuff in space. Whitehead was concerned with the order of nature as though the relations are fundamentally spatial. The motivation is to be as simple and unified as possible, so long as the "limited number of propositions . . . concerning our sense-perceptions" are sustained. The classical conception required not only *points of space* but *particles of matter* and *instants of time.* What we have then as the basis of a science of nature is geometry, chronology, and dynamics. Because this concept "demands two classes of objective reals," presumably particles of matter over against points of space and instants of time, it "will be called . . . *Dualistic.* . . ." Although the work is one in mathematical physics, it has a basic philosophic motivation, to find "a concept which demands only one such class [which] will be called . . . *Monistic* . . ." (*MCMW,* 14–15). Occam's Razor is invoked to justify a simplification as an "instinctive preference." The way this can be accomplished is shown by Leibniz, who made space relational. Whitehead does not ascribe to Leibniz the concept of real particles essentially related temporally, which latter-day concept is, in his judgment, "a protest against exempting any part of the universe from change" (*MCMW,* 14).

The importance of this conception of nature is that there must be orders of the points, in the sense of serial order, or a relation that is transitive, asymmetrical, and connected. Perhaps we can grasp the most significant foundation of a polyadic relation in his analysis of "The Essential Relation." This is "a pentadic relation, and has for its field both the class of instants of time and that of linear objective reals, that is . . . the field is the complete class of ultimate existents. The proposition R: *(a b c d t)* can be read as the statement that *the objective real a intersects the objective reals b, c, d in the order bcd at the instant t.* This conception of 'the intersection in order of three linear objective reals by a fourth at an instant of time' must be taken as a fundamental relation between the five entities" (*MCMW,* 34). The "real" is here most clearly defined in terms of orders. This is a complete break with those traditions in philosophy which define the real as something unrelated, or as sometimes defined, "substance" or "absolute."

It must not be thought, because of this emphasis on orders that define the real, that the view is of a static world. Motion is measured by reference to "kinetic axes." The objective reals are in motion and "we require a kinematical science for linear objective reals in this concept analogous to the kinematical parts of hydrodynamics" (*MCMW,* 43; cf. 60). This world is then clearly one of becoming and passing away, a world of transience, like water, and classically expressed by Heraclitus: "all flows." Whitehead does not use the classical model of Heraclitus, who is conceived to be the metaphysical opposite of Plato. But if this view includes both the Platonic pole of forms of definiteness and Heraclitean pole of process, then the metaphysical significance of this memoir, read before the Royal Society in

London in 1904, and published in 1906, may be the conceptual integration of what had been hitherto considered incompatible.

Further developments of nature as events in time, a process, in terms of orders, are contained in *The Principles of Natural Knowledge* (1919) and *The Concept of Nature* (1920). These more sustained analyses of events in space and time attempt, rather than formalization as mathematics, to show such concepts "rooted in experience."[5] ". . . The scientific concepts of space and time are the first outcome of the simplest generalizations from experience, and they are not to be looked for at the tail end of a welter of differential equations" (*PNK,* vi). Because it is an effort "to explain special laws of nature," we are referred to many philosophers of the past and present who have stimulated the work, as well as to Einstein and others whose theory of relativity then demanded attention (*PNK,* vii–viii). In the second edition we are promised "a more complete metaphysical study" (*PNK,* ix).

The fundamental conviction of Whitehead's cosmology is that nature is a cosmos. This conviction of Pythagoras, that man inhabits an ordered whole that can be made intelligible, has become so widespread that almost every succeeding philosophy takes it for granted. Whitehead makes explicit philosophy's search for a unifying concept. To seek for "relations" is

an ideal in the absence of which philosophy must languish from lack of intrinsic interest. That ideal is the attainment of some *unifying concept which will set in assigned relationships within itself all that there is for knowledge, for feeling, and for emotion.* That far off ideal is the motive power of philosophic research; and claims allegiance even as you expel it.[6]

The emphasis Whitehead gave to this ideal shows that he clearly identifies philosophy with the search for order, for to "set in assigned relationships within itself" is a broad definition of order, and a better one than that of serial order.

We must examine kinds of order, such as those that are symmetrical, as equivalence, as well as those that are asymmetrical, for both would be "assigned relationships." That is, such a conception would include both $a = b, b = c \therefore a = c$ even though $=$ is symmetrical, for the terms may be exchanged, as they cannot be $1 < 2, 2 < 3, \therefore 1 < 3$. Here, $<$ is to be read "is less than."

Even those philosophies which stress relative disorder still are committed to cosmos. Some emphasize a world of many things, of contradictions, or rule of arbitrary will of God or fate, or ever-changing situations with problems. "The philosophic pluralist is a strict logician; the Hegelian thrives on contradictions by the help of his absolute; the Mohammedan divine bows before the creative will of Allah; and the pragmatist will swallow anything so long as it 'works'!" (*CN*, 2). It is challenging to consider whether more extreme protests against traditional concepts of a rational order also reaffirm cosmos.

The problem Whitehead faces, rather than doing a dialectical critique of other philosophies, is that presented at the beginning of this chapter. Experience does not directly disclose a cosmos. Actual experience is of flux, "disorderly . . . fragmentary, and with elements not clearly differentiated." The question is not whether there is a unity of science, which the philosophy of the sciences endeavors to exhibit, but in what sense nature is a system apart from what we think of it (*CN*, 1–2). Although our science "is exclusively concerned with homogeneous thoughts about nature," what of the heterogeneous nature "which we observe in perception through the senses?" (*CN*, 3).

Confront nature itself as you experience things in relation, and forget your science and your religion and all else you have been taught to think, and say whether it is a cosmos or a system. This is a realistic imperative, and when honest, "nature" is taken as "closed" in the sense that its relations "do not require the expression of the fact that they are thought about." Not only is this nature as sensed, the nature so considered is "the terminus of sense-perception," and natural science is "not concerned with the sense-awareness itself" (*CN*, 3–4). The closure is also to exclude any "disjunction of nature and mind," and "any reference to moral or aesthetic values whose apprehension is vivid in proportion to self-conscious activity" (*CN*, 4–5).

The Principles of Natural Knowledge and *The Concept of Nature* are very complex and it is easy to stray into the many byways, but the answer to the problem is made clear. Experienced nature *is* a cosmos because the events encountered are spatially and temporally related. The "ultimate facts of nature, in terms of which all physical and biological explanations must be expressed, are events connected by their spatio-temporal relations, and . . . these relations are in the main reducible to the property of events that they can contain (or extend over) other events which are parts of them" (*PNK*, 4).

We have no experience of anything in a durationless moment, and what we experience ultimately as an event must "include the notion of a state of change" (*PNK*, 2). Not only is there extension or "spread through space" but "functioning takes time" (*PNK,* 3). Although the argument is said not to be metaphysical, it does concern what is "the ultimate fact," or the real (*CN,* 15). There is an "it" to which different observers can point, but this is not accurately or helpfully characterized as a "substance." The reason is that when we distinguish the individual real thing, calling it "this" or "that," we also must in experience include some ambiguous reference to what it is, not merely that it is. Yet this does not justify characterizing the attributes as predicates because there are relations as well as properties. That is to say, the real is not so much a "substratum" of qualities as a "situation." "If we are to look for substance anywhere, I should find it in events which are in some sense the ultimate substance of nature" (*CN,* 6–19).

Thus Whitehead resolves the first difficulty in bringing order out of the disorder we experience. We can differentiate elements yet recognize that they occur in a situation or a context.

The next point beyond distinguishing things is complementary: we encounter and experience "things as related" (*PNK,* 13). Each of us knows himself perceiving something in nature. Just as above we saw a rejection of the idea of an unrelated substance, so here the rejection of what such a view implies: that our minds introduce all relations. Other predecessors had indeed held that there were no relations between things without our comparing one to another. Whitehead inspects his experience and invites us also to consult ours.

How are events related among themselves? More fundamental than either spatial or temporal relations is extension. By analyzing experience we discover a way events may be found in various relations of inclusion or exclusion.

Events are the relata of the fundamental homogeneous relation of "extension." Every event extends over other events which are parts of itself, and every event is extended over by other events of which it is a part. The externality of nature is the outcome of this relation of extension. Two events are mutually external, or are "separate," if there is no event which is part of both. Time and space both spring from the relation of extension. Their derivation will be considered in detail in subsequent parts of this enquiry. It follows that time and space express relations between events. (*PNK,* 61)

Here is an application of the broader definition of "order," to "set in assigned relationships within itself." If Boston is separate from Washington, then Washington is separate from Boston. The relation is mutual: we can treat the terms as symmetrical and reverse them. But there is an asymmetry in the part-whole relation: if Capitol Hill is a part of Washington, then Washington, as a whole, cannot be part of Capitol Hill.

Of utmost importance in unifying our conception of nature, assuring us of cosmos, is the celebrated "Method of Extensive Abstraction." This is one of the most explicit applications of the logic of relations and the definition of serial order as a relation that is transitive, asymmetrical, and connected. The relation K stands for "extends over." If $a\,K\,b$ and $b\,K\,c$, then $a\,K\,c$. If $a\,K\,b$ then not $b\,K\,a$. Whitehead's demonstration could also say either $x\,K\,y$ or $y\,K\,x$, where x and y are any two terms in the field of K (PNK, 101). Whitehead does add the concept of "abstractive class" of events, of which "of any two of its members one extends over the other." There is an added stipulation, which is: "There is no event which is extended over by every event of the set" (PNK, 104).

The properties of an abstractive class secure that its members form a series in which the predecessors extend over their successors, and that the extension of the members of the series (as we pass towards the "converging end" comprising the smaller members) diminish without limit; so that there is no end to the series in this direction along it and the diminution of the extension finally excludes any assignable event. Thus any property of the individual events which survives throughout members of the series as we pass towards the converging end is a property belonging to an ideal simplicity which is beyond that of any one assignable event. There is no one event which the series marks out, but the series itself is a route of approximation towards an ideal simplicity of "content." The systematic use of these abstractive classes is the "method of extensive abstraction." All the spatial and temporal concepts can be defined by means of them. (PNK, 104)

We now have a solution to the problem of points of space, and also instants of time as well. There is an illustrative help provided by Whitehead: a series of Chinese boxes, illustrating the argument that conceivably there could be no least, but only a limit. To get to a line the concentric series of rectangles are diminished from opposite sides. They tend to zero width (PNK, 105).

Thus "abstractive elements," which are used in science, are deduced from the experience of extension, and in this way we have a route from untidy experience to the neat world of science. Whitehead as other scientists often talks of connecting the rough and the smooth. Although we do not directly experience such ideal limits as points and lines, we experience planes of volumes. Yet he can conclude that

An abstractive element will be said to "inhere" in any event which is a member of it. Two elements such that there are abstractive sets covered by both are said to "intersect" in those abstractive classes. One abstractive element may cover another abstractive element. The elements of the utmost simplicity will be those which cover no other abstractive elements. These are the elements which in euclidian phrase may be said to be "without parts and without magnitude." (*PNK*, 109)

Once again, there is recognition of both symmetry and asymmetry in dimensions of the order of nature. In "the passage of events is extension in the making. The terms 'the past,' 'the present,' and 'the future' refer to events. The irrevocableness of the past is the unchangeability of events. An event is what it is, when it is, and where it is" (*PNK*, 62). This is the basis of asymmetry in our experience and in nature, particularly based on *passage of events* or what is later called process. The extreme contrast is to "objects" which we already introduced by a later name "eternal objects," the forms of definiteness or possibles, which are also later characterizations of the respects in which we recognize sameness in events. These are the factors in fact.

If events are the extreme example of asymmetry, objects are the extreme example of symmetry. Asymmetry is a recognition of such difference that one term cannot be set in reverse relation to another, but symmetry is a recognition that similarity, like quantitative equality, is a recognition of sameness such that one term can be set in reverse relation to the other.

Objects enter into experience by recognition and without recognition experience would divulge no objects. Objects convey the permanences recognized in events, and are recognized as self-identical amid different circumstances; that is to say, the same object is recognized as related to diverse events. Thus the self-identical object maintains itself amid the flux of events: it is there and then, and it is here and now; and the "it" which has its being there and here, then and now, is without equivocation the same subject for thought in the various judgments which are made upon it. (*PNK*, 62–63)

Because the object is "permanent" it is "without time and space; and its change is merely the variety of its relations to the various events which are passing in time and in space" (*PNK*, 63).

Events in time call our attention to "the directional factor in time which expresses that ultimate becomingness which is the creative advance of nature" (*PNK*, 63).

There are many complexities encountered in these studies of the order of nature. One such is that there is no one absolute time. There are, rather than one, many time-systems. Each reveals certain characteristics of the passage of events. By refusing the bifurcation of nature into the relative and the absolute or what is "individual experience and external cause," the consequence is reassuring of the authenticity of our experience, that there is some doubt about the "consistency for all."[7] This is one of the themes developed a few years after *The Concept of Nature* in *The Principle of Relativity* (1922).

In defending the unity of nature Whitehead goes further in defending the cosmos. Nature excludes mind and is whatever we perceive. "For natural philosophy everything perceived is in nature. We may not pick and choose. For us the red glow of the sunset should be as much part of nature as are the molecules and electric waves by which men of science would explain the phenomenon" (*CN*, 29). What is hereby denied is

the bifurcation of nature into two systems of reality, which, insofar as they are real, are real in different senses. One reality would be the entities such as electrons which are the study of speculative physics. This would be the reality which is there for knowledge; although on this theory it is never known. For what is known is the other sort of reality, which is the byplay of the mind. Thus there would be two natures, one is the conjecture and the other the dream (*CN*, 30)

Can there be a coherent unity of nature that includes mind? Can knowledge be conceived without the notion of something outside, that can be the cause in us of an idea? Whitehead admits the great difficulty of his own conception of thought as "an interaction within nature," particularly when nature is conceived as adventures of matter in space and time (*CN*, 31). The commitment he has made to demonstrating cosmos seemed to demand a sharp break, not only from the main doctrines of modern science inherited from Newton, but also the main implications as drawn by Locke and his followers.

Although "nature" had been defined as closed to mind, and also closed to moral and aesthetic value, nevertheless, it is now conceived to include mind. And there is one strong hint of what is subsequently developed as the value intrinsic to actuality. This is the "significance." Although we perceive the room, there is "a world beyond the room to which our sight is confined, known to us as completing the space-relations of the entities discerned within the room." From one perspective, is this the "ragged edge" of nature, without a sharp division between what we discriminate and what we do not discriminate (*CN*, 50)? Yet from another perspective this is a "disclosure of an entity as a relatum" and "the basis of our conception of significance." There are other entities that do not necessarily enter consciousness. "Thus significance is relatedness, but it is relatedness with the emphasis on one end only of the relation" (*CN*, 51). We may not at this time suppose that Whitehead intended this "more," as yet unknown, to be something beyond nature; but it is a dim awareness of the whole of nature present in a part. However we discriminate nature into parts, there is yet the implication that they are parts of a whole. "There is the part which is the life of all nature within a room, and there is the part which is the life of all nature within a table of the room" (*CN*, 74). The author is not convinced that the prejudices inculcated by language, formal teaching and convenience can be trusted to rule out the significance of what is commonly expressed in poetry. In the succeeding book, *The Principle of Relativity*, the chapter on "The Relatedness of Nature" begins: "Threads and floating wisps of being . . ." (*R*, 13).

Beyond this somewhat mystical import, another question to raise is practical. What is the use or application of this mathematics or logic to an order of nature? If we turn from *The Principles of Natural Knowledge* or *The Concept of Nature* to *An Introduction to Mathematics*, we find geometry defined as "the science of dimensional order," a division of "the more general science of order" (*IM*, 181). The subject has "real bearing" when we consider our assumption of continuity. It is not merely that light coming from the sun is "a continuous function of the time" that passes.

Consider a train in its journey along a railway line, say from Euston Station, the terminus in London of the former London and North-Western Railway. Along the line in order lie the stations of Bletchley and Rugby. Let *t* be the number of hours which the train has been on its journey from Euston, and *s* be the number of miles passed over. Then *s* is a function of *t*, i.e., is the variable value corresponding to the variable argument *t*. If we know the circumstances of the train's run, we know *s* as soon as any special value of *t* is given. Now, miracles apart, we may confidently assume that *s* is a continuous function of *t*. It is impossible to allow for the contingency that we can trace the train continually from Euston to Bletchley, and that then, without any intervening time, however short, it should appear at Rugby. The idea is too fantastic to enter into our calculation: it contemplates possibilities not to be found outside the *Arabian Nights;* and even in those tales sheer discontinuity of motion hardly enters into the imagination, they do not dare to tax our credulity with anything more than very unusual speed. But unusual speed is no contradiction to the great law of continuity which appears to hold in nature. (*IM*, 111)

That nature is cosmos is then worked out on the basis of experience, with the use of logic and appeals to the results of science. But these are evidently not sufficient for Whitehead. He added the appeal of "significance" and the argument that there is no sincere alternative belief to that by which we live.

The Mechanistic Order of Nature

Whitehead's conceptions of the order of nature were not completed with the three works sometimes referred to as those of his period of philosophy of science, though the works are better regarded as philosophy of nature because they are less epistemological than cosmological. He had given us strong hints of dissatisfaction with the tradition of physical science as well as with its philosophy. He had moved from considering nature as matter in space to events temporally related. This move was forced upon him by the inconsistency of a scientific scheme that tried to account for motion at a durationless moment. The crisis of the new relativity theory connected with the genius of Einstein had turned Whitehead to reading Galileo to discover how modern physics had begun. But there was no promise of a study such as *Science and the Modern World,* which is an historical account of the mechanistic order of nature and which we can consider in this section, to be followed by an alternative in the next section, the organic order of nature. The accounts of these divergent theories have become classic, and are developed from a critical and constructive stage into the metaphysical system of *Process and Reality,* in which what we take to be central is "The Order of Nature." Two lectures are published in *Modes of Thought,* "Nature Lifeless" and "Nature Alive," and these strongly reinforce the forking of the road. If, as our last section concluded, the acceptance of nature as cosmos is as certain as any fundamental belief can be, which of the several concepts of that order, with different conceptions of law of nature, does the evidence lead us to prefer?

The mechanistic scheme, developed as the foundation of modern science since 1600 by Galileo, Kepler, Newton, and their followers, is a triumph of abstract intelligence. Whitehead never tires of calling our attention to the abstraction of the few simple categories: particles of matter in space with the simple pushes and pulls that philosophers call efficient causes.

. . . We can conceive nature as composed of permanent things, namely bits of matter, moving about in space which otherwise is empty. . . . A bit of matter is thus conceived as a passive fact, an individual reality which is the same at an instant, or throughout a second, an hour, or a year. Such a material, individual reality supports its various qualifications such as shape, locomotion . . . etc. The occurrences of nature consist in the changes in these qualifications, and more particularly in the changes in the qualifications, and more particularly in the changes of motion. The connection between such bits of matter consists purely of spatial relations. (*MT,* 174–75)

The conception of homogeneous space is clarified in geometry, particularly developing the theory of points, lines, surfaces, etc.

The appeal of such a scheme is to commonsense observation. This is "the world as interpreted by reliance on clear and distinct sensory experiences . . ." and it is the world presupposed in legal theory, in which there is "the enduring self-identity of a house," etc. (*MT,* 174). Because it can be applied in ordinary life, Whitehead cannot but affirm it

because in some sense it is true. There are bits of matter, enduring self-identically in space which is otherwise empty. Each bit of matter occupies a definite limited region. Each such particle . . . has its own private qualification, such as its shape, its motion, its mass. . . . Some of these qualifications change, others are persistent. The essential relationship between bits of matter is purely spatial. Space itself is eternally unchanging, always including in itself this capacity for the relationship of bits of matter (*MT,* 179).

To examine this theory of the Order of Nature, Whitehead gives an account of its origin, development, and consequences. This is a history of mechanism. He also gives an internal analysis of the concepts. This is a logic of mechanism. He also considers the relations of the categories of mechanism to other categories of existence. This is a criticism of mechanism. By following history, logic, and criticism, we can appreciate the depth and scope of his appraisal.

When in *Introduction to Mathematics* Whitehead told of the new epoch of the seventeenth century, with the simultaneous invention by Newton and by Leibniz of the differential calculus, he was moved to quote a passage from Shelley.

> The sun-awakened avalanche! whose mass,
> Thrice sifted by the storm, had gathered there
> Flake after flake,—in heaven-defying minds
> As thought by thought it piled, till some great truth
> Is loosened, and the nations echo round.

The poetic analogy is apt because a new method uses the materials that have long and gradually gathered.

. . . Some genius by the invention of a new method or a new point of view, suddenly transforms the whole subject to a higher level.

The comparison will bear some pressing. The final burst of sunshine which awakens the avalanche is not necessarily beyond comparison in magnitude with the other powers of nature which have presided over its slow formation. The same is true in science. The genius who has the good fortune to produce the final idea which transforms a whole region of thought does not necessarily excel all his predecessors who have worked at the preliminary formation of ideas. In considering the history of science, it is both silly and ungrateful to confine our admiration with gaping wonder to those men who have made the final advances towards a new epoch (*IM,* 162)

When in *Science and the Modern World* Whitehead picked up the theme as "The Century of Genius" he wrote his own poetry: "Since a babe was born in a manger, it may be doubted whether so great a thing has happened with so little stir" (*SMW,* 3).

The "order of nature in modern thought" is a vision provided by ancient fate, a "remorseless working of things." In contrast to "moral order" this "remorseless inevitableness is what pervades scientific thought. The laws of physics are the decrees of fate" (*SMW,* 15, 16). Because of scholastic logic this belief was interpreted to mean "that every detailed occurrence can be correlated with its antecedents in a perfectly definite manner, exemplifying general principles" (*SMW,* 18). But only after the "over-theoretical" Greeks and the "rationalistic" medievals, in the latter Renaissance, were these principles reduced to a "naive faith" and applied to "irreducible and stubborn facts" (*SMW,* 22–24).

The old foundation of science is a "happy choice" from the categories of Aristotle's successors: "irreducible brute matter, or material, spread throughout space in a flux of configurations. . . . It does just what it does do, following a fixed routine imposed by external relations which do not spring from the nature of its being" (*SMW,* 25). The scheme was very efficient in calling "attention to just those groups of facts which, in the state of knowledge then existing, required investigation" (*SMW,* 26). The method was a revolt against the rationalism that ignored brute fact.

Then the analysis of the rise of modern science requires the Pythagorean emphasis on numbers, not only arithmetic but the further generalization, algebra. What was so very powerful was the construction for every relationship conceivable in the "full universe," of formulas "without any specification of particular entities." Only *x, y, z* are stated to ensure complete generality (*SMW*, 38–39). These are the arguments of the function or the variables, and a powerful way of specifying the order of nature (*SMW*, 45–46).

. . . This dominance of the idea of functionality in the abstract sphere of mathematics found itself reflected in the order of nature under the guise of mathematically expressed laws of nature. Apart from this progress of mathematics, the seventeenth century developments of science would have been impossible. Mathematics supplied the background of imaginative thought with which the men of science approached the observation of nature. Galileo produced formulae, Descartes produced formulae, Huyghens produced formulae, Newton produced formulae. (*SMW*, 46)

The account of the rise of modern science is paradoxical. Can a method be both of the "utmost abstractions" and also pertinent to "concrete fact" (*SMW*, 48)? This is exactly what the most effective thought must be, according to Whitehead, for only the most abstract can apply to all the specific instances discovered. ". . . In thus becoming abstract it became useful" (*SMW*, 48, of trigonometry, but applicable to all mathematics). The paradox is removed if the most abstract is the most general and that means to refer to all cases.

Galileo applied mathematics in measuring the rate of falling bodies and producing a formula. The basis was provided for Newton.

The common measurable element of *mass* was discerned as characterizing all bodies in different amounts. [Also later it is added, "Mass remained permanent during all changes of motion."] Bodies which are apparently identical in substance, shape, and size have very approximately the same mass. The closer the identity, the nearer the equality. The force acting on a body, whether by touch or by action at a distance, was [in effect] defined as being equal to the mass of the body multiplied by the rate of change of the body's velocity, so far as this rate of change is produced by that force. In this way the force is discerned by its effect on the motion of the body. The question now arises whether this conception of the magnitude of a force leads to the discovery of simple quantitative laws involving the alternative determination of forces by circumstances of the configuration of substances and of their physical character. (*SMW*, 66–67)

The resulting "three laws of motion and . . . the law of gravitation" have survived the tests and the "cumulative triumph has been the whole development of dynamical astronomy, of engineering, and of physics" (*SMW*, 67).

The last point is that this is "an ideally isolated system." By this is meant isolation "within the universe," or "freedom from casual contingent dependence upon detailed items within the rest of the universe," but "only in respect to certain abstract characteristics . . . and not in respect to the system in its full concreteness" (*SMW*, 68).

Whitehead's text is difficult to follow because along with his history and analysis he introduces a third perspective on the mechanistic order of nature. This is criticism, which, developed over a period of twenty years, reaches a climax in *Science and the Modern World* (1925) and is reinforced in "Nature Lifeless" (1933, later reprinted in *Modes of Thought* [1938]).

The first main point of criticism is that the mechanistic order of nature is abstract. This has been illustrated in many ways, particularly in the quantitative concepts that are required by the methods of measurement. But if nature is the whole object of our sense experience, our sight, touch, hearing, taste and smell, this means that in science we have substituted our conception of this order for what we grasp directly, and this means that there is always more in experience than can be presented in the laws. Whitehead had begun his criticism of the abstraction of science by admitting in *The Concept of Nature* that the order of nature meant the "multiple relations between . . . factors" which are "posited in the sense awareness of nature," excluding the ultimate character of reality (*CN*, 151). But there is also the exclusion of life and mind from what is considered the phenomenal range of experience, not only the metaphysical concern with the status of eternal objects and the problem of a ground of order. There are indeed objects that recur, but no consideration of the relation of one recurrence, say red, to another recurrence, say sphericity. Whitehead had shown a use of poets in several writings before *Science and the Modern World,* but nothing comparable to "The Romantic Reaction." The chapter on "The Century of Genius" ends with the results of mechanical science: "Nature is a dull affair, soundless, scentless, colorless; merely the hurrying of material, endlessly, meaninglessly" (*SMW*, 80). However, efficient and without serious rival as "a system of concepts," the view of modern science is "quite unbelievable" (*SMW*, 80).

The logical error involved in taking mechanical order to be the order of nature is to "have mistaken our abstraction for concrete realities." (*SMW*, 81). Mistaking the abstract for the concrete is called the "Fallacy of Misplaced Concreteness" (*SMW*, 75).

The explanation of how we fall into fallacy requires the contrast between Whitehead's analysis of experience in the "act of perception" to the traditional view that the object perceived, say green, is simply a quality of the leaf. This of course has led to the problem that the sensation depends on being sensed, and therefore that the green is not in the leaf at all. Perception requires both perspectives, and in the act is in an "interlock [ing] plurality of modes" (*SMW,* 102–3).

Thus if green be the sense-object in question, green is not simply at A where it is being perceived, nor is it simply at B where it is perceived as located; but it is present at A with the mode of location in B. (*SMW,* 103)

Everyone who has been introduced to a philosophic problem knows the question whether there is a sound when a tree falls unobserved. Under those circumstances, there can be no "prehension," or a "gathering of things into the unity of a prehension." There can be no reference *here* and *now* to some other place and time (*SMW,* 101–2).

There is no particular mystery about this. You have only got to look into a mirror and to see the image in it of some green leaves behind your back. For you at A there will be green; but not green simply at A where you are. The green at A will be green with the mode of having location at the image of the leaf behind the mirror. Then turn round and look at the leaf. You are now perceiving the green in the same way as you did before, except that now the green has the mode of being located in the actual leaf. (*SMW,* 103–4)

Is it a description of what we do experience that every sense object, such as green is "expressible as located [for "location"] elsewhere?" (*SMW,* 104).

One very interesting truth is about sound, and a point applicable to sight. ". . . Sound is voluminous: it fills a hall, and so sometimes does diffused color" (*SMW,* 104).

When so regarded, "nature" and "experience" are, as in the philosophy of John Dewey, brought very close together: "The actual world is a manifold of prehensions . . ." (*SMW,* 104).

Another fallacy, closely associated with misplaced concreteness, is "simple location." This property of *here* or *there* refers equally to both space and time, and means that to explain a thing means there is no need to refer "to other regions of space-time" (*SMW,* 72). The modern view of all nature at an instant of time could develop because, in distinction to dividing space, which does divide the material, to divide a portion of time does not divide the material. Thus one may conclude that "the lapse of time is an accident, rather than of the essence, of the material" (*SMW,* 73).

The mechanistic order of nature also is a case of extreme dualism, or what Whitehead called "The Bifurcation of Nature." The bifurcation referred to is best known as the theory of "primary and secondary qualities." Whitehead understands John Locke to mean that "there are some attributes of the matter which we do perceive. These are the primary qualities, and there are other things which we perceive, such as colors, which are not attributes of matter, but are perceived by us as if they were such attributes. These are the secondary qualities . . ." (CN, 27). To this Whitehead's response is "Why should we perceive secondary qualities? It seems an unfortunate arrangement that we should perceive a lot of things that are not there" (CN, 27).

The ground of criticism is that called epistemological realism: our "sense-awareness is an awareness of something" (CN, 28). Rather than a theory of a psychic addition that is made by our minds, this realism has objects which allow real relations between the things known.

Another way of stating the objection is that the nature characterized scientifically is regarded as the cause of the nature which we perceive. But this divides the world into "two systems of reality." The abstract world is never directly known, only postulated, hence is a world of conjecture, and what it is supposed to explain is a world of dream (CN, 30).

What is needed is not a rejection of either the theoretical order of nature or the perceived order of nature, but relating one to the other in a comprehensible way. That is, the theoretical order is of "abstractions from more concrete elements of nature, namely from events," and what is abstracted includes space and time, and what is real is relational. Thus Whitehead corrects the Lockean view that it is only "the orderliness of these [spatio-temporal] relationships [that] constitutes the order of nature" (SMW, 79).

The implication of the mechanistic world is that perceived qualities other than the quantitative are "purely the offspring of the mind. Thus nature [in the common sense view as opposed to the mechanistic] gets credit which should in truth be reserved for ourselves: the rose for its scent: the nightingale for his song: and the sun for his radiance." If mechanism were right, then "the poets are entirely mistaken. They should address their lyrics to themselves, and should turn them into odes of self-congratulation on the excellence of the human mind" (SMW, 80).

Apart from these fallacies of reasoning in using the modern mechanical order as a cosmology and the dualism there is one cosmological belief that introduces incoherence into the Newtonian system. This is the view that the order of nature is primarily spatial, and that natural order can be understood at a temporal moment. Whitehead was familiar with Bergson's view that real time had been ignored and that what philosophers meant by "time" was only the clock time of theoretical physics. That is, philosophy had replaced the reality with the measurement. Whitehead "agree[d] with Bergson in his protest [against the "spatialization" of time]" but it is "not necessary that the intellect fall into the trap, though in this example there has been a very general tendency to do so" (*SMW,* 74–75). For there to be motion, even merely locomotion, requires a spread of time, which Bergson called duration.

In several ways the inadequacy of the whole mechanistic scheme, however successful as science, shows up beyond cosmology in the metaphysical situation. The methodological limitation of nature to what is perceived, with which Whitehead agreed in the *Concept of Nature,* became the metaphysical doctrine that over against *matter* is

mind, perceiving, suffering, reasoning, but not interfering. [This belief] has foisted onto philosophy the task of accepting [them] as the most concrete rendering of fact.

Thereby, modern philosophy has been ruined. It has oscillated in a complex manner between three extremes. There are the dualists, who accept matter and mind as on equal basis, and the two varieties of monists, those who put mind inside matter, and those who put matter inside mind. But this juggling with abstractions can never overcome the inherent confusion introduced by the ascription of *misplaced concreteness* to the scientific scheme of the seventeenth century. (*SMW,* 82)

The fundamental matter-mind dualism omits the intermediaries between the extremes. "In between there lie the concepts of life, organism, function, instantaneous reality, interaction, order of nature. which collectively form the Achilles heel of the whole system" (*SMW,* 84). By "order of nature" the text means more than the abstract Newtonian scheme. And how are we to confront nature in "concrete experience"? As the poets do, and the testimony of Shelley and Wordsworth "emphatically bear witness that nature cannot be divorced from its aesthetic values . . ." (*SMW,* 127).

If one objects that he or she is not romantic in feeling the presences throughout the whole of nature, as Wordsworth reports in "Tintern Abbey," the "sense of something far more deeply interfused," then the

argument becomes one of whose intuition to trust. Whitehead clearly
distrusts the mind that confines "attention to a definite group of abstractions" and has only thoughts of "clear-cut definite things, with clear-cut
definite relations" (SMW, 85). There is an alternative: "Wordsworth's
'presence that disturbs me with the joy of elevated thoughts. . . .'"

Perhaps Whitehead has Bertrand Russell in mind when he remarks:
"We all know those clear-cut trenchant intellects, immovably encased in a
hard shell of abstractions. They hold you to their abstractions by the sheer
grip of personality" (SMW, 85). This is "one-eyed reason, deficient in its
vision of depth" (SMW, 86). Whitehead knows the gratitude we owe to
these eighteenth-century haters of injustice and obscurantism, but on
balance stresses the limitations of Voltaire. ". . . If men cannot live on
bread alone, still less can they do so on disinfectants" (SMW, 87).

This defense of the "romantic" against the "rationalist" (in the
eighteenth-century sense) could be met, as it was by Russell, who replied,
according to legend, "I'd rather be narrow-minded than vague and
woolly." Whitehead has one final argument against the mechanistic
scheme of Newtonian physics:

. . . The development of natural science has gradually discarded every single
feature of the original commonsense notion. Nothing whatever remains of it,
considered as expressing the primary features in terms of which the Universe is
to be interpreted. (MT, 177)

Whitehead writes with peculiar intensity about the presuppositions of
modern science because he had been taught to believe them as absolute
truths. When he write of how science has abandoned empty space, inert
particles of matter, external relations, and imposed law, he is writing of his
own loss of old scientific faith. Happily he writes from the perspective of
having gained a new faith.

The notion of empty space, the mere vehicle of spatial interconnections, has
been eliminated from recent science. The whole spatial universe is a field of
force, or in other words, a field of incessant activity. (MT, 186)

Matter has been identified with energy, and energy is sheer activity; the
passive substratum composed of self-identical enduring bits of matter has been
abandoned, so far as concerns any fundamental description. Obviously this
notion expresses an important derivative fact. (MT, 188)

The evidence is not only from physics, but also from biology; and since
organisms are more concrete and more integrated units of activity, this

evidence may be more important. The genes were once considered unalterable "determinants of heredity." But if they were conceived on analogy to atoms, the thought is now, why not generalize from genes, and conceive atoms on analogy to genes? "Thus no *a priori* argument as to the inheritance of characters can be drawn from the mere doctrine of genes. In fact recently physiologists have found that genes are modified in some respects by their environment" (*MT*, 190)

What follows from the "modern point of view . . . of energy, activity, and the vibratory differentiations of space-time"? Nothing less than internal relations, a doctrine of absolute idealism, and the romantic experience of the whole in the part: "Any local agitation shakes the whole Universe. The distant effects are minute; but they are there. . . . The group of agitations which we term matter is fused into its environment. There is no possibility of a detached, self-contained local existence. The environment enters into the nature of each thing" (*MT*, 188).

And what now are the laws of nature? The "forms of process" (*MT*, 192). ". . . The laws of nature are merely all-pervading patterns of behavior, of which the shift and discontinuance lie beyond our ken" (*MT*, 196). This concept is otherwise called immanent law, and because dependent upon interrelated events, subject to change. The laws then cannot be eternally the same, but are subject to systematic alteration, however slight. The laws we know can therefore be only the laws of our epoch.

And what is nature? "Nature is a theatre for the inter-relations of activities. All things change, the activities and their inter-relations" (*MT*, 191–92).

In reaching the conclusion, Whitehead expresses agreement with the great absolute idealist of Oxford, F. H. Bradley, author of *Appearance and Reality*. Nature is "activities and process. What does this mean? These activites fade into each other. They arise and then pass away. What is being enacted? What is effected? It cannot be that these are merely the formulae of the multiplication table—in the words of a great philosopher, merely the bloodless dance of categories. Nature is full-blooded. Real facts are happening" (*MT*, 197).

Although the modern order of nature began with a reaffirmation of ancient fate, the deepest shift from mechanism may well be the denial of necessity ruling over all events and the affirmation of freedom of each to be what it is and to pursue its own end. "All realization involves implication in the creative advance" (*MT*, 200).

Chapter Four

The Order of Experience: From Nature Dead to Nature Alive—Part Two

Organic Mechanism

There have been many philosophers critical of mechanism and many philosophers supportive of organicism. Whitehead will probably emerge as the most subtle because even in developing "the philosophy of organism," he defended "the theory of *organic mechanism.*" What is true in mechanism? On a lower level with regard to parts it is not wrong. "In this theory, the molecules may blindly run in accordance with the general laws, but the molecules differ in their intrinsic characters according to the general organic plans of the situations in which they find themselves" (*SMW*, 116).

The entities influence one another and are modified by their environment. This is one of a number of striking differences between organicism and mechanism, based upon the organism as "a unit of emergent value, a real fusion of the characters of eternal objects, emerging for its own sake" (*SMW*, 157). If mechanism has interchangeable units, practically indistinguishable, each of the realities of organicism has a uniqueness. The order is therefore expressed as an envisagement which includes a degree of freedom and purpose throughout nature.

It is even possible that [physical entities] may be developed into individualities of more fundamental types, with wider embodiment of envisagement. Such envisagement might reach to the attainment of the poising of alternative values with exercise of choice lying outside the physical laws, and expressible only in terms of purpose.

Apart from such remote possibilities, it remains an immediate deduction that an individual entity, whose life-history is a part within the life-history of some larger, deeper, more complete pattern, is liable to have aspects of that larger pattern dominating its own being, and to experience modifications of that larger pattern reflected in itself as modifications of its own being. This is the theory of organic mechanism. (*SMW*, 156)

We shall follow the pattern used above for mechanism. That is, we shall develop it historically and analyze its major concepts. But since the tests do not criticize organicism as mechanism is criticized, we shall diminish this phase to an elaboration of the theory and its application.

These qualifications should always be kept in mind. On some levels mechanism is not false, and on these levels organic freedom and purpose may be developed. The opposition between mechanism and organicism is not then exclusive, as are fully contradictory propositions not both of which may be true.

Organic Order of Nature

It is conceivable that real things attract and repel one another, in contrast to the principle of mechanism that there is merely "passive matter . . . operated on externally by forces." This possibility of organicism was expressed by the philosopher credited in the modern world with the inductive methods of modern empiricism, Francis Bacon. Whitehead found in him a line of reasoning that modern science completely overlooked. Bacon generalizes the situation of magnetism. ". . . As when the loadstone draweth iron" so "all bodies whatsoever . . . elect . . . to embrace that which is agreeable, and to exclude or expel that which is ingrate . . ." (*SMW*, 61, 60). Whitehead comments on this passage of "Natural History" of *Silva Silvarum* that this basically organic conception makes life the fundamental truth about bodies (*SMW*, 61).

Whitehead generalizes even beyond Bacon. Bacon says of all bodies that "though they have no sense, yet they have perception." That is, though only some bodies have *"cognitive experience,"* all *"tak*[*e*]. . . *account* of" one another. This is, says Whitehead, a more fundamental truth than the materialist way of regarding matter as passive because such matter is utterly opposed to mind, and there is no link between the two (*SMW*, 60 ff.).

Traditional theories of knowledge attempted to account for cognition on the basis of sense-perception. The body was regarded as the passive recipient of sense impressions. What is lacking is the turning of body to the light. We observe this in the tropism of plants (*S*, 42). Because we

have neglected the fact that our encounter "involves emotion, and pur-
pose, and valuation, and causation," a new term is needed (*PR*, 28).
Prehending is the "gathering of things into . . . unity . . ." (*SMW*, 101).
By "unity" is meant that prehensions cannot be torn out of context. There
is a process from prehension to prehension. . . . The *reality is the process*
(*SMW*, 106, italics added).

Here is the best hint of his project which took five more years to
complete, *Process and Reality* (1929). The title is an answer to F. H.
Bradley's *Appearance and Rality*. In this masterpiece of idealism, it is mind
that constitutes reality. Whitehead proposes a realism of events that,
because of organic relations, has all the advantages of stating how nature is
a whole. It is also called "philosophy of process." As a philosophy that
accounts for knowledge, it offers a solution to the problem for which Bacon
is best known, what is called "induction." Sometimes this is stated as the
problem of reasoning from particular instances to general laws. Bacon held
"the belief that with a sufficient care in the collection of instances the
general law would stand out by itself" (*SMW*, 63). Whitehead regards this
account as "inadequate," apart from the obvious logical fallacy of drawing
a universal conclusion from a particular premise, or generalizing from
"some" members of a class to "all" members of that class. The deeper
problem, according to the philosophy of organism, is how to infer "from
particular occasions in the past to particular occasions in the future"
(*SMW*, 64). It is therefore essential to think of reality as process. Only if
from "the immediate occasion, as set before us in direct cognition" we
know past and future, can the problem be solved.

Either there is something about the immediate occasion which affords knowledge of the past and the future, or we are reduced to utter scepticism as to
memory and induction. (*SMW*, 64)

The concrete event of organicism has a future as well as a past. "A mere
abstract" of "material objects in a flux of configurations in time and space"
could tell us "only that they are where they are" (*SMW*, 64). But this
metaphysical approach gives us "knowledge that there *is* a future already
subjected to some determinations" (*SMW*, 65).

An event has contemporaries. This means that an event mirrors within itself the
modes of its contemporaries as a display of immediate achievement. An event
has a past. This means that an event mirrors within itself the modes of its
predecessors, as memories which are fused into its own content. An event has a

future. This means that an event mirrors within itself such aspects as the future throws back on the present, or, in other words, as the present has determined the future. (*SMW*, 106–7)

Therefore to know an event is to make it possible to foretell its future, for the "event has anticipation." Whitehead has then a real basis for prophecy, a word which he uses in poetic quotation. Exactly what tests we use to check the truth of predictions is not made clear. The only great exception is that whatever is to come is within some "order of nature." What will occur is not governed by any necessary laws, but by patterns which develop out of the past into the present and beyond into the future.

The philosophy of organism is then a statement of an evolutionary order.

Let us grant that we cannot hope to be able to discern the laws of nature to be necessary. But we can hope to see that it is necessary that there should be an order of nature. The concept of the order of nature is bound up with the concept of nature as the locus of organisms in process of development. (*SMW*, 108)

Evolutionary order, "the emergence of novel organisms," is coupled with the notion of "permanence [of energy] underlying change" (*SMW*, 147). Together these strengthen the view of nature as process, which is a concrete unity in contrast to the merely conceptual unity of mechanism" (*SMW*, 107). This is based on the coupling of change and endurance, even the acceptance of both chance and endurance, even the acceptance of both chance and regularity (*SMW*, 126, 147). Whereas mechanism tends to be deterministic and to relegate alleged cases of "chance" to the subjective status of "ignorance," this alternative organicism has the advantage of accepting chance as real. Sometimes followers of Whitehead develop these hints into a full-fledged "indeterminism."

Whitehead's argument is that energy and electromagnetic fields provide the physical conception of a nature in which biological organisms are not an exception. Without this continuity of the physical and the biological, there might have to be the discontinuity of a vitalism that, although it has to accept mechanism, accounts for life by some vital principle which is completely an exception to the physical order of nature (*SMW*, 150).

The conservation of energy provided a new type of quantitative permanence. It is true that energy could be construed as something subsidiary to matter. But, anyhow, the notion of *mass* was losing its unique preeminence as being the one final permanent quantity. Later on, we find the relations of mass and energy inverted; so that mass now becomes the name for a quantity of energy considered in relation to some of its dynamical effects. (*SMW*, 149)

Not only can energy be fundamental, but also "energy is merely the name for the quantitative aspect of a structure of happenings; in short, it depends on the notion of the functioning of an organism" (*SMW*, 149).

The same relegation of matter to the background occurs in connection with the electromagnetic fields. The modern theory presupposes happenings in that field which are divorced from immediate dependence upon matter. (*SMW*, 149)

Not only is ether unnecessary for the theory, but "the atom is transforming itself into an organism; and finally the evolution theory is nothing else than the analyses of the conditions for the formation and survival of various types of organisms" (*SMW*, 149).

Science as a whole, then, is the study of organisms, and the distinction between physics and biology is that physics studies smaller organisms whereas biology studies larger organisms. Whitehead speculates further about continuity. Biological organisms include the smaller physical organisms, and perhaps "the smaller of the physical organisms can be analyzed into component organisms." However, "it seems very unlikely that there should be any infinite regress in nature." Then there must be some primary entity, and the name Whitehead gives to this "ultimate unit of natural occurence" is the "event" (*SMW*, 150–51).

Organicism is characterized as a "non-materialistic philosophy of nature" because the primary organism is defined as "the emergence of some particular pattern as grasped in the unity of a real event" (*SMW*, 151). At this point it is necessary to consider the relation of eternal objects to actuality. The relation of an event to "all there is, and in particular with all other events" is "effected by the aspects of those eternal objects, such as colors, sounds, scents, geometric characters, which are required for nature . . ." (*SMW*, 151). These enter into the event because they qualify another event. Because these aspects are related there are patterns. "Each event corresponds to two such patterns; namely, the pattern of aspects of other events which it grasps into its own unity, and the pattern of its aspects which other events severally grasp into their unities" (*SMW*, 151). This is a kind of reciprocity of every event, partially determined by other events, and partially determining other events. "There is thus an intrinsic and an extrinsic reality of an event, namely the event as in its own prehension, and the event as in the prehension of other events" (*SMW*, 151). This is a most important way to elaborate what we saw earlier as the characterization of the real as relational rather than substantial, and crucial to the development of a metaphysics of order.

One difficulty encountered in the debates between idealists such as Bradley and realists such as Russell was whether there can be more than one reality. For if there is "the interaction of organisms," there might be one interrelated whole, one organism (*SMW*, 151). To maintain a plurality of real events or organisms, it becomes necessary to make a distinction between the "real togetherness" in the pattern of an event and the "logical togetherness of merely diverse things." These "things" are the eternal objects and they are not "alike one to another" (*SMW*, 152).

The philosophy of organism diverges most sharply from mechanism in the status of value and purpose. Whereas mechanism rules out value and purpose from nature, and the only place for them must be the mind, even the narrowly human, the organic conception finds a necessary place for value in nature. Whitehead counters "nature is valueless" with a proposition calculated to shock the materialist: "the actuality is the value" (*SMW*, 155). But if we have followed Whitehead so far we must consider his argument. The actuality is a selection and unification of the possibilities open for actualization. Therefore "the emergence of organisms depends on a selective activity which is akin to purpose." Then, since the organism is only partly determined by "the general state of the universe," the organism can be said to be "emerging for its own sake" (*SMW*, 156, 157). What underlies such a process? There is a daring metaphysical assertion:

The consideration of the general flux of events leads . . . into an underlying eternal energy in whose nature there stands an envisagement of the realm of eternal objects. . . . In the nature of the eternal activity there must stand an envisagement of all values to be obtained by a real togetherness of eternal objects, as envisaged in ideal situations. Such ideal situations, apart from any reality, are devoid of intrinsic value, but are valuable as elements in purpose. (*SMW*, 154)

It is difficult to read this without wondering what it is that it is envisaging and what role such a being has in aiding the selection for realization. Whitehead's texts are full of suggestions that God immanent in the world is necessary to make process intelligible.

The eternal objects, this passage makes clear, are not good in themselves, but good only for actualities. Knowing that they are of value is reserved for thought of "subtler and more complex enduring patterns." But all actualities as individualized have some value, whether they are conscious of this value or not. The philosophy of organism has broken with the classical Platonistic tradition of ascribing supreme good to the ideal apart from actualization in process, and it has broken also with the subjectivism that would rest value and purpose on mind divorced from nature. Organicism is then somewhere in the middle between extreme value realism and value subjectivism.

"According to this theory the evolution of laws of nature is concurrent with the evolution of enduring pattern" (*SMW,* 156). Organicism again breaks with the mechanistic concept of cosmic determinism. Newton had the Lord God impose eternal and unchanging necessities upon nature. As to aggregations, the effects are such that we must take them into account in formulating causal regularities. "Accordingly, the characteristic laws of inorganic matter are mainly the statistical averages resulting from confused aggregates" (*SMW,* 162). This is the clearest statement of agreement with Charles Sanders Peirce that disorder can be a form of order. But this is a special case when "organic unity fades into the background" (*SMW,* 161). Since for Whitehead all actualities are patterned and present "aspects which are there for prehension," the "laws" are the constancies dependent upon the patterns and relations between actualities. "The laws of physics represent the harmonized adjustment of development which results from this unique principle of determination" (*SMW,* 155). The important words "harmonized adjustment" indicate another divergence from classical mechanism. According to mechanism "evolution . . . is reduced to . . . another word for the description of the changes of the external relations between portions of matter. There is nothing to evolve, because one set of external relations is as good as any other set of external relations. There can be merely change, purposeless and unprogressive" (*SMW,* 157).

To derive the more complex from antecedent states of the less complex requires an organic conception of creative advance. The process, developing enduring patterns, allows between them a relation of "more, or of less, importance" (*SMW,* 158). Matter is no longer fundamental. "Nature . . . comprises enormous permanences." Thereby endurance is no longer "an arbitrary fact at the base of the order of nature . . ." (*SMW,* 159–60). The traits making for endurance, such as cooperation of organisms with one another and with a favorable environment, introduce further value factors into the evolutionary order (*SMW,* 160). It is always assumed that life is on the whole better than nonlife. Hence we have the basis of an ethics laid in the order of nature. This we shall develop below as Whitehead's anticipation of ecology. Survival value is read from Whitehead's book of nature: "If organisms are to survive, they must work together" (*SMW*, 160). "Any physical object which by its influence deteriorates its environment, commits suicide" (*SMW*, 161).

Whitehead's use of biological concepts in developing the philosophy of organism raises a most interesting question. If physics was the most advanced science of the seventeenth century and the model for chemistry and biology as they developed in the eighteenth century, is it now biology that is to be taken as paramount? The philosophy of organism, in Whitehead's case, is not based on this judgment. He used not only theory of evolution but theory of energy and romanticism in poetry as well. He strengthens his case in *Science and the Modern World* with chapters on twentieth-century physics, particularly the chapter "Relativity," to show that although scientists still profess much of the old mechanism, the new concepts fit into the organic theory of nature (*SMW*, 173ff.).

A full account should be based on Whitehead's *The Principle of Relativity with Applications to Physical Science* of 1922 and various related essays on Einstein and "Space, Time and Relativity," but the argument in *Science and the Modern World* is sufficient.

Twentieth-century physics no longer uses the old absolute space and absolute time of Newton. "The new relativity associates space and time with an intimacy not hitherto contemplated; and presupposes that their separation in concrete fact can be achieved by alternative modes of abstraction, yielding alternative meanings" (*SMW*, 173).

It is the new physics that is organicist not only in making space-time relative to events, but in considering them as patterns "reproduced in each temporal slice of its history" (*SMW*, 174).

Relations take on greater importance and it is crucial to see the idealist "internal relations" affirmed, but with qualification.

. . . The relatedness of an event [is] all internal relations, so far as concerns that event, though not necessarily so far as concerns the other relata. For example, the eternal objects, thus involved, are externally related to events. This internal relatedness is the reason why an event can be found only just where it is and how it is,—that is to say, in just one definite set of relationships. For each relationship enters into the essence of the event; so that, apart from that relationship, the event would not be itself. This is what is meant by the very notion of internal relations. (*SMW*, 179–80)

Whitehead knows well the battle Russell fought with Bradley's doctrine of internal relations. The argument establishes unique individuality on this basis to avoid the charge that there can be on this theory only one reality and that we cannot know anything without knowing everything. Below we shall see another qualification, the sense in which there are some "spatio-temporal relationships" that are external or at least refer to independence of events, namely when they are contemporary.

In the context of the new physics it can be said that "internal relations require the concept of substance as the activity synthesizing the relationships into its emerging character" (*SMW*, 180).

There is on this view of process no conceivable way to think of time and space as extensions composed of extensionless moments and points. This generated the famous paradoxes of Zeno to prove that there can be no change since the number of such moments and points is infinite and cannot be traversed. Time and space are continuities not enclosed within limits and without smallest parts. Hence the new physics avoids paradox.

Realization is the becoming of time in the field of extension. Extension is the complex of events, *quâ*: their potentialities. In realization the potentiality becomes actuality. (*SMW*, 185)

The concept of temporalization is not of complete continuity because there are the permanences of events.

Temporalization is not another continuous process. It is an atomic succession. Thus time is atomic (i.e., epochal), though what is temporalized is divisible. (*SMW*, 185)

This is a crucial modification of the concept of the order of nature. Without it, there would be no place for any such discontinuities affirmed by quantum theory.

It is then not necessary to begin with biology to arrive at an organic conception of nature. Whitehead gives his personal testimony. "In fact by reason of my own studies in mathematics and mathematical physics, I did in fact arrive at my convictions in this way" (*SMW*, 219).

A real individual is not a mere "habitat of energy" but an "organizing activity, fusing ingredients into a unity, so that this unity is the reality" (*SMW*, 221,224). Because events are interdependent, and so constitute "the enduring organism," there is order, but more complex than abstract serial order. Organic order is always in contrast to disorder. "There can be no peculiar meaning in the notion of 'order' unless this contrast holds" (*PR*, 127).

Whereas the serial order of mathematics and the efficient order of mechanism assume no end or goal, the terms of organic order are "adaptation for the attainment of an end" (*PR*, 127). It is common to use order as reference to arranging parts directed to a single end, but this is specifically denied. To comprehend how the order of nature can be purposive, but with many final ends, we must turn to the causal order.

The Causal Order of Nature

In discussing the order of nature, Whitehead's conceptions moved from spatial ordering to temporal ordering, and with prehension, the transmission of energy, and the patterning of events, *Science and the Modern World* prepared for the order of nature as a causal order. A year after its publication came *Symbolism: Its Meaning and Effect*. The second of these lectures given at the University of Virginia is about causal efficacy. This in particular is a continuation of the criticism of the adequacy of mechanism and an endeavor to defend a philosophy of organism. But, as in the formula of organic mechanism, the philosophy is to include in a synthesis all that is true in the traditional world view of modern science. The emphasis on causal efficacy continues in *Process and Reality*, "Symbolic Reference" (*PR*, 255–79), and in the dominant theme of "Nature Alive," a lecture at the University of Chicago (*MT*, 202–32).

One passage in the premetaphysical works indicates why Whitehead came to discuss experience and causality together. This is a statement in *The Concept of Nature*, in Chapter 1, of the insoluble status of knowledge in a nature conceived as "two systems of reality." On the one hand there is causal interaction within nature, such as burning heating a body, but then there is only the appearance which has an influence on "the alien mind which thereupon perceives redness and warmth" (*CN*, 31). The difficulty is that the preconception of knowledge is that "mind can only know that which it has produced and retains in some sense within itself, though it requires an exterior reason both as originating and as determining the character of its activity." The problem is to find a single system of relations in which to locate both "causal interaction within nature" and the mind's knowledge. The problem at that time seemed to be solved by a space-time order (*CN*, 32–33).

From the perspective of mechanism Whitehead had not ignored causality because he had worked out a theory of temporal succession, and the prevailing concept of causality, achieved by Hume, had reduced cause and effect to a succession of states. Whitehead agreed with the deduction of this theory from Newtonian mechanism because this excluded mind, as well as life, from nature. If mind is but the spectator of the world, the relationship of causality is undiscoverable from sense impressions. This reduces mind to "the familiar immediate presentation of the contemporary world." There are in experience only "impressions" as Hume called them, or "sense data" as Whitehead's friend Russell called them. Whitehead goes to Hume for the classic description of "mere passive admission of the impressions through the organs of sensation . . .; in none of them can the mind go beyond what is immediately present to the sensor, either to discover the real existence or the relations of objects" (Hume, *Treatise*, Part 3, Section 2, quoted in *S*, 32). Whitehead calls this the mode of "Presentational Immediacy."

This account of experience is limited to "the contemporary world," and not only is such experience "vivid" but sharp and clear in a way exalted in modern philosophy. It "is especially distinct in its exhibition of the spatial regions and relationships within the contemporary world" (*S*, 14).

Although contemporaries are independent, such as the "percipient at that moment" and the wall, for example, with its color and extensiveness, according to this reading of experience, there is a concrete relationship between them. This is "relevance amid independence" because the relation "may be very unessential to the wall and very essential to the percipient" (*S*, 15–16).

Is our experience limited to the mode of presentational immediacy? This is the test case of the viability of the philosophy drawn from modern science. If what we have from experience is images, then there is no difference between "the image of a colored chair, presenting to us the space behind the mirror" and "an immediate presentation of color qualifying the world at a distance behind the mirror, as is our direct vision of the chair when we turn round and look at it" (*S*, 24).

The conclusion drawn is that we either have an image or we do not, an application of the all or none principle. We are like the dog in Aesop's fable "who dropped a piece of meat to grasp at its reflection in the water" (*S*, 19).

"Pure presentational immediacy refuses to be divided into delusions and not-delusions. It is either all of it, or none of it, an immediate presentation of an external contemporary world as in its own right spatial" (*S*, 24).

But we are not, as Aesop's dog, poor thinkers because we use our sense data as related to a wider "world than these contemporary things can express" (*S, 24*). We bring things together in symbolic reference, and we are not content with the barrenness of mere appearance. This is a most interesting way of raising the question of our judgments of what is real.

"Our experience, so far as it is primarily concerned with our recognition of a solid world of other things which are actual," is itself actual in "the same sense that we are actual . . ." (*S, 17*). The situation of an organism in its environment is not that of mind having appearance, but "our most immediate environment is constituted by the various organs of our own body, our more remote environment is the physical world in the neighborhood" (*S, 18*). Through our bodies we encounter "the qualities of the actual things" (*S, 21*).

If we have "direct experience of an external world," then this is of an enduring organism in a world of organisms. Each has a life history, or a past and future as well as a present. In this world there are active agents and the world is "an interplay of functional activity" (*S, 28–29*).

Experience, from the perspective of organicism, is activity. It is "self-production" and production of objects, for which we are responsible as the "potter, and not the pot, is responsible for the shape of the pot" (*S, 8–9*). This activity is also a source of information about the world, and the problem is what we learn in this mode that we do not learn by presentational immediacy, and how the two ways together tell us about the same world (*S, 30*).

Since Whitehead's perceptive mode "Causal Efficacy" is presented as a challenge to the exclusive use of "Presentational Immediacy," he is contrasting them in ways other than awareness in activity of process including past and future rather than perception of the present only. Although the present images are vivid and clear in spatial relationships, they tend to be trivial. And though we do not have precise access to past and future, and the information is vague, it is important for all agents to know the sequence of events. The examples of the relevance of the future are from animal as well as human behavior. A dog anticipates "the immediate future to his present activity with the same certainty as a human being" (*S, 42*). A person in the dark has, in absence of clear impressions, a "terrifying sense of vague presences, effective for good or evil over fate" (*S, 43*). The images of the present may be "handy and definite in our consciousness" and easy to reproduce, but it is the "vauge, haunting, unmanageable" that is insistent (*S, 43*).

Causal efficacy includes emotional response, such as "anger, hatred, fear, terror, attraction, love, hunger, eagerness, massive enjoyment" (*S, 45*). Whitehead is one of the few philosophers in deepest sympathy with

William James's stress on the emotions. Whitehead espouses "the prag-matic aspect of occurrences. . . ."

> These primitive emotions are accompanied by the clearest recognition of other actual things reacting upon ourselves. The vulgar obviousness of such recogni-tion is equal to the vulgar obviousness produced by the functioning of any one of our five senses. When we hate, it is a man that we hate and not a collection of sense-data—a causal, efficacious man. (S, 45)

Although the dog fails in making remote inferences, we have this capacity and exercise it without doubt. Whitehead's example is that of dynamite exploding.

> If dynamite explodes, then present fact is that issue from the past which is consistent with dynamite exploding. . . . We unhesitatingly argue backwards to the inference. . . . If dynamite be now exploding, then in the immediate past there was a charge of dynamite unexploded. (S, 46)

The example could be used of our fear and precautions when dynamite and a charge of electricity are brought together as conditions of a future explosion.

Time, according to the mode of presentational immediacy, is "pure succession," which omits activity. The following passage can be made more intelligible by recalling the prehension of the past, and unification of its patterns.

> Time is known to us as the succession of our acts of experience, and thence derivatively as the succession of events objectively perceived in those acts. But this succession is not pure succession: it is the derivation of state from state, with the later state exhibiting conformity to the antecedent. Time in the concrete is the conformation of state to state; the later to the earlier; and the pure succession is an abstraction from the irreversible relationship of settled past to derivative present. (S, 35)

Whitehead might have added, since there are only particular pasts to which particular careers must conform, that to take the asymmetrical order of succession to be real time is another example of the fallacy of misplaced concreteness. By the primacy of causal order nature is a succes-sion of events.

Whitehead recognizes that the orders considered in mathematics are abstracted and unreal in themselves.

> The integers succeed each other in one way, and events succeed each other in another way; and, when we abstract from these ways of succession, we find that pure succession is of the second order, a generic abstraction omitting the temporal character of time. . . . (*S,* 35)

Are there fixed conditions to which acts must conform? There is an expression, "stubborn fact," that shows our common apprehension of this ordering of nature. Whereas in Hume's analysis, "there are no stubborn facts," the philosophy of organism appeals to facts against Hume's argument (*S,* 37).

But could not real time be a contribution of the mind? The Kantian view is just as fallacious as the Humean view. For Kant accepted Hume's view of particular facts as "simple occurrences." Rather than the "simple location" of something that "simply happens," there is experience of the relation of obligation. This is the obligation "every particular actual thing lays upon the universe . . . of conforming to it." This is the form of "universal truths [that] are discoverable" (*S,* 39). Whitehead is as wary of stating such general truths as he is of stating axioms of inference. Perhaps he considered it just too obvious that an event cannot precede itself, that a future or potential consequence cannot be a past actuality, etc. Later he put such a truth: "No thinker thinks twice; and, to put the matter more generally, no subject experiences twice" (*PR,* 43).

If we experience the structure of nature, then there is no need to try, as did Hume, to account for causal efficacy as a habit of thought or, as did Kant, to call it a category of thought (*S,* 39–40). The experience is unlike Hume's characterization of vivid impressions, or Kant's account of sensation. But there is certainty in the experience of conformation (*S,* 41–42). Whitehead had in *Symbolism* worked his way back from modern subjectivism that makes problematic (to state the problem in the words of Russell's celebrated book) our knowledge of the external world. Not only did Whitehead revert to pre-Kantian realism but to a position that justifies the use of Plato, Aristotle, and the medievals in his realism. But the reversion is more profoundly to primitive experience, the grasp of reality shared by humans with other animals. There is an order of nature in which animals can find prey, and after the hunt, take the food home to the cubs.

The clear conclusion of *Symbolism* is that what we do grasp through causal efficacy is the structure of events or a causal order of nature:

The bonds of causal efficacy arise from without it. They disclose the character of the world from which we issue, an inescapable condition round which we shape ourselves. . . . Our natures must conform to the causal efficacy. (*S*, 58)

The contrasts between presentational immediacy and causal efficacy are made even sharper in *Process and Reality*. A theory of the body and feelings is elaborated to sustain the emphasis on causal efficacy. We see with our eyes, etc. and this is called "withness of the body"; and "feeling the body as functioning" gives us not only "this body is *mine*," but "this actual world is mine" (*PR*, 125–26). The theory of feelings includes the analysis of the subject's response to an objective datum, such that the "cause is objectively in the effect . . ." (*PR*, 363).

"Feeling" is extended throughout the world and causality is everywhere present. ". . . A simple physical feeling is the most primitive type of an act of perception, devoid of consciousness" (*PR*, 361). Again of this "most primitive perception": it is the "feeling of the body as functioning" and of "the world in the past" (*PR*, 125). Further there is here in language from "higher stages of experience," what we call "*sympathy*, that is, feeling the feeling *in* another and feeling conformally *with* another" (*PR*, 246).

Although earlier we heard that experience in the mode of causal efficacy was vague where presentational immediacy is precise, when we respond bodily to threat we take the position of other bodies into account. Art is "symbolic transfer of emotions," immediately presented, and so powerful is music that we may pay no attention to spatial arrangements of the players. Local relations of an orchestra are important only for our hearing of music.

We do not listen to the music in order to gain a just appreciation of how the orchestra is situated. When we hear the hoot of a motor car, exactly the converse situation arises. Our only interest in the hoot is to determine a definite locality as the seat of causal efficacy determining the future. (*S*, 84)

It is a project for us to observe also whether we block out the color and shape when we attend to the place and attend also to the direction and speed of the vehicle. This would be an example of our feeling for the vector character of bodies in motion (*PR*, 268).

Because, in Whitehead's correct judgment, philosophers have "disdained the information about the universe obtained through their visceral feelings, and have concentrated on visual feelings," he makes a great point of the importance of "'feeling' throughout the actual world" (*PR*, 184, 268). Although feelings are vague, they suffice for animals, plants, and even lower forms of organic life. There must be "feeling of causal nexus, although we" cannot ascribe "definite percepts" to the jellyfish as it advances and withdraws and the plant's roots grow down in the soil and the leaves tend upward toward the sun (*PR*, 268). This passage is of peculiar significance because it shows Whitehead shifting away from a dichotomy toward degrees of an hierarchical scale. It is also a case of finding reason in nature, and the ground for human reasoning in causal relationship.

Not only are causal relationships found throughout nature, but also inwardly in memory and in continued activity. Why is memory in the mode of causal efficacy? ". . . Memory is perception relating to the data from some historic route [or chain of transmission relating to the data from] percipient subjects M_1, M_2, M_3, etc., leading up to M which is the memorizing percipient" (*PR*, 184). Related to memory is the "canalization of the creative urge." Here the appeal is to stubborn fact or common sense.

> . . . We essentially arise out of bodies which are the stubborn facts of the immediate relevant past. We are also carried on by our immediate past of personal experience; we finish a sentence *because* we have begun it. The sentence may embody a new thought, never phrased before, or an old one rephrased with verbal novelty. There need be no well-worn association betwen the sounds of the earlier and the later words. But it remains remorselessly true, that we finish a sentence *because* we have begun it. We are governed by stubborn fact. (*PR*, 197)

Past philosophers have missed "immediate transition" because they had concentrated on remote consequences and scientific induction.

Another problem for presentational immediacy is how we can perceive any difference between past and future and any temporal direction. Without "direct perception of those antecedent actual occasions which are causally efficacious" we cannot have the perception of direction. In presentational immediacy there is only past and future "indirectly perceived by means of their extensive relations to the presented locus" (*PR*, 256–57).

We not only have two modes of perception which are contrasted, but two modes that make up for each other's deficiencies and can be harmonized. *Process and Reality* gives a fuller account by far of the harmony.

There is between the two pure modes a common ground in the presented locus. Although this is vague for causal efficacy, it is made more precise by the spatial dimensions clear to presentational immediacy. But we add to three spatial dimensions the "fourth dimension of temporal thickness 'spatialized' as the specious present of the percipient" (*PR*, 257). In the percipient the "perspectives are focused . . ." and we gain the complete determinate scheme of extensive regions (*PR*, 257).

Another way in which the two modes harmonize is to consider both of them in relation to the perception of eternal objects. We are then using a third mode, "conceptual analysis." We not only get to "abstract attributes, qualities and relations" from the "actual things of the actual world" which we perceive passively but also actively (*S*, 17). This is the second common ground for the symbolic reference that connects the two modes. Certainly a third mode with something in common would serve to combine them (*PR*, 259).

Another common ground is the identity of the datum. "The two modes express the same datum under different proportions of relevance" (*PR*, 262). Different sorts of integrations are possible. One of the most interesting examples is the phenomenon of blinking when, in the dark, the electric light is suddenly turned on. In the mode of presentational immediacy there is the "flash of light, feeling of eye-cloture, instant of darkness." These are practically simultaneous. There is also perception in the mode of causal efficacy. "He feels that the experiences of the *eye* in the matter of the flash are causal of the blink. The man himself will have no doubt of it" (*PR*, 265). Only because of the latter mode can a man say that the flash happened prior to the blinking, and the "flash to blink" sequence is a feeling of which we are sure (*PR*, 266).

What we express in terms of "the stone is grey," a substantive and an adjective, is derived from two modes. ". . . The substantives convey our dim percepts in the mode of efficacy." ". . . 'Grey' refers to the grey shape immediately before our eyes. . . ." The British empiricists had become increasingly dubious of the first mode, and tended to eliminate it. The grey shape is indeed "definite, limited, controllable, pleasant, or unpleasant . . ." (*PR*, 272). But it is through efficacy that process philosophy restores substance to empirical philosophy, with the importance of "reference to past [and] to future" (*PR*, 272).

The two modes enter into "the experiential process" in temporal sequence. There is first "the responsive phase, and [then] the 'supplemental' phase. . . . The mode of efficacity belongs to the responsive phase, in which the objectifications are felt according to their relevance in the datum: the mode of immediacy belongs to the supplemental phase in which the faint indirect relevance, in the datum, of relationships to regions of the presented locus are lifted into distinct, prominent, relevance" (*PR, 273*).

When we have synthesized the two modes in symbolism, there is a great difference between the modes of expression. One mode is of "sound, the rhythmic relations of the component sounds, the intensity of the sound." Then the words are "euphonious or harsh, concordant or discordant with other accompanying sounds." This is in the perceptive mode of immediacy (*PR, 276*). The other mode in which we respond to symbols is as meanings. To grasp the correlation by a "ground" of relatedness, there is dependence on the experiential process. Could this be without efficacy (*PR, 276*)? There is, however different the sound and the meaning, a common test. The symbolism is "right or wrong" and the test, as well as the justification, is pragmatic. The "very meaning of truth is pragmatic." But this can work only because for some occasion there is a "definite determination of what is true on that occasion. Otherwise the poor pragmatist remains an intellectual Hamlet, perpetually adjourning decision of judgment to some later date" (*PR, 275*).

As to causal efficacy we find a further advance in "Nature Alive." Among the reinterpretations of causal efficacy is a development of the charge that if we rely on presentational immediacy alone we tend toward the atomic independence of impressions, or experience as a shower of atoms, reported by Hume. Explanation depends on finding some ground of "understandable causation," and not, even in science, merely "a formula for succession" (*MT, 202*). Fruitful hypotheses come through the perception of reasonable connections. Although the apprehension is dim, to pursue such a causal relation is fruitful. The justification then is pragmatic. "For example, the observation of insects and flowers dimly suggests some congruity between the natures of insects and of flowers, and thus leads to a wealth of observation from which whole branches of science have developed" (*MT, 203*). To be content with the bare facts of "insects visiting flowers" would be a positivistic failure to develop civilization.

What now stands out about a living being effecting changes is "self-enjoyment, creative activity, aim" (*MT, 208*).

Here "aim" evidently involves the entertainment of the purely ideal so as to be directive of the creative process. Also the enjoyment belongs to the process and is not a characteristic of a static result. The aim is at the enjoyment belonging to the process. (*MT, 208*)

Just as causal efficacy was introduced with an example from productive activity, the potter responsible for the shape of the pot, so the theme is climaxed with the conception of "creative advance." This is ascribed to the universe, of "the essence of the universe," and not merely to the human craftsman (*MT*, 207). Nature as a causal order is also a creative order. There is no longer a "sharp division between mentality and nature" in our experience. ". . . Mental occurences are operative in conditioning the subsequent course of nature" (*MT*, 214).

This leads to a conclusion that the duality between soul and world is transcended. We saw earlier that "experience" has so broad a meaning that it is finally indistinguishable from "nature." Here it is the mutual immanence of "the stream of experience" and "the external world" (*MT*, 223).

. . . The experienced world is one complex factor in the composition of many factors constituting the essence of the soul. We can phrase this shortly by saying that in one sense the world is in the soul. But there is an antithetical doctrine balancing this primary truth. Namely, our experience of the world involves the exhibition of the soul itself as one of the components within the world. (*MT*, 224)

Does the world include the soul or the soul the world? The relation of including runs both ways. This symmetry is illustrated. ". . . I am in the room, and the room is an item in my present experience. But my present experience is what I now am" (*MT*, 224). Whitehead allows that this is a "baffling anthetical relation." A way to remove the paradox is to consider that the body is shared by the person experiencing and the world experienced. ". . . The world for me is nothing else than how the functioning of my body presents it for my experience. The world is thus wholly within those functionings." Alone this would be a radical subjectivism. "And yet, on the other hand, the body is merely one society of functionings within the universal society of the world" (*MT*, 225). This alone would be an objectivism or a naturalism. We shall later see a metaphysics that pushes both the truth of subjectivism and objectivism but holds them together in tension.

The Hierarchical Order of Nature

The most important mode of order affirmed by Whitehead, as a result of the shift in cosmology from mechanism to organicism, is that Nature is a hierarchy. In place of the sharp dualism between two forms of substance, thinking substance and extended substance, or mind and matter, Whitehead affirms a continuum with no "sharp division between mentality and nature." The most explicit summary is from *Modes of Thought*.

A rough division can be made of six types of occurrences in nature. The first type is human existence, body and mind. The second type includes all sorts of animal life, insects, the vertebrates and other genera. In fact all the various types of animal life other than human. The third type includes all vegetable life. The fourth type consists of the single living cells. The fifth type consists of all large scale inorganic aggregates, on a scale comparable to the size of animal bodies or larger. The sixth type is composed of the happenings on an infinitesimal scale, disclosed by the minute analysis of modern physics. (*MT*, 214–15)

This is a rough classification, and we might expect the scientist in Whitehead to make it sharp. This he refuses to do for several reasons. One is methodological: "sharp-cut scientific classifications essential for scientific method . . . are dangerous for philosophy." The second reason is that the organic truth about Nature is that "all these functionings influence each other, require each other, and lead on to each other." To be true to the forms, between animal and vegetable for example, we should have far more than six, even an infinity.

Whitehead then restates the hierarchical scheme with an emphasis on the principle by which animal is ranked higher than plant and cell ("central direction") and the organic above inorganic (activity and freedom versus "passive acceptance of necessities"), and the inorganic above the inframolecular (passivity on larger or smaller scale). The analysis is incomplete, but noticeably there is no dominating stress on power, which is used so frequently in such schemes to place man highest as the dominant species. The order of forms of life is exciting because of what it does not say, as well as because of what it says:

There is the animal life with its central direction of a society of cells, there is the vegetable life with its organized republic of cells, there is the cell life with its organized republic of molecules, there is the large-scale inorganic society of molecules with its passive acceptance of necessities derived from spatial relations, there is the infra-molecular activity which has lost all trace of the passivity of inorganic nature on a larger scale. (*MT*, 215)

If there was a gradual emergence of the living from the nonliving, there is the problem of what in the nonliving enabled the living to emerge.

Whitehead's hierarchical order has the advantage of an organic continuity in which there is no sharp boundary. ". . . There is no absolute gap between 'living' and 'non-living' . . ." (PR, 156).

Then we would have to restate the concept of "type" above. It is not so much a difference of kind as a difference of degree. The highest order is mental, with fullest access to the eternal objects, and therefore more free to choose from them what is to be actualized. Therefore we should expect Whitehead to ascribe to the highest the maximum of creative innovation.

Does "higher than" reduce, as in some analyses of hierarchical order, to "more complex than," as in the gradation of eternal objects? It is possible to think of the higher level as more inclusive than the lower level, and since atomic elements enter into molecules, and molecules into cells, cells into organs, organs into organisms, that we could assert simply that the higher has all the characteristics of the lower, plus some differentiae not present in the lower. But since this would attribute mentality only to man, the highest, and Whitehead wants no such gulf between man and the animal, this seems to be one respect in which he diverges from an Aristotelian classification of types of being. Rather than more complexity, it is suggested that we look to the functioning of a higher being, both in terms of novelty and order. Both are required for genuine creativity, and the ordering of life is to an end which the higher animal sets for itself. There is then more the kind of hierarchy of souls, as in ancient and medieval philosophy. The higher is the more active, the lower the more passive.

In its lowest form, mental experience is canalized into slavish conformity. It is merely the appetition towards, or from, what already is. The slavish thirst in a desert is mere urge from intolerable dryness. This lowest form of slavish conformity pervades all nature. It is rather a capacity for mentality, than mentality itself. But it *is* mentality. . . . It produces no disturbance of the repetitive character of physical fact. It can stretch out no arm to save nature from its ultimate decay. It is degraded to being merely one of the actors in the efficient causation.[1]

Arguments often rest on the distinction between "high-grade" and "low-grade" organisms, and some such hierarchy is presupposed. Probably because of the danger of dualism, which was for Whitehead a problem to be solved, his emphasis is on the continuity of the grades rather than the distinction between them. But in a theory of experience, it is necessary to say that "presentational immediacy is only of importance in high-grade organisms. . . ." Knowledge itself remains a fusion of "physical experience and conceptual imagination" (*S*, 16). The importance of complexity on the higher level is that it provides a "variety of sense-presentation." Thereby comes vivid distinctness of presentational immediacy. But the fact of being higher and rather rare means that it is developed later in the evolutionary process, but there is no reason whatsoever for despising and neglecting the more primitive (*PR*, 263ff.). Perhaps another reason why Whitehead has a hierarchical order of nature without much emphasis on it is that readers would have mistaken it as an evaluative scheme rather than as a description of the way organisms are. Whitehead makes clear that he opposes reductionism in the sense of reducing all spirit to matter, or all organic relations to a mechanical order. He does after all recognize, as in traditional Aristotelian philosophy, formal and final causes as well as material and efficient causes. The problem is to have a scheme adequate to the complexity; and many traditional hierarchical schemes, as in the Plotinian tradition of Neo-Platonism, have "reduction" in reverse. That is the opposite fallacy of deriving all the lower levels from the higher, and reducing plurality to some aboriginal unity. With the acceptance of the evolution of higher from lower forms rather than reverse, it is a problem of delicate adjustment of evolutionary order to hierarchical order.

The shock of evolution to Victorian consciousness came as a rude denial of the dignity of man. If Darwin was right, then Genesis was wrong. No longer could it be said that "man was in the image of God," but rather a higher ape. The philosophy of organism is not a device for rescuing a theological view of man from the pits of scientific materialism. Rather Whitehead recognized that accompanying a demonstrable "higher" status was a responsibility of a more demanding sort. Man's knowledge and power, if they are not to be destructive of nature, must be guided and directed. Hence the philosophy of organism saves what is important for conduct in the traditional view without entering into the insoluble problem created by the Victorians and still troublesome when stated as one authority against another.

What is man's place in the hierarchy of nature? In several respects his position as the highest animal can be argued from what has been developed. As an animal he has a "central direction" because of his nervous system, and the direction to ends that are conceived as universally valid goals gives to man a godlike status. When he directs his efforts to truth, beauty, adventure, peace, as we shall see in the next chapter, then he has, as God, a graded envisagement of the good. Whitehead, because of a grading of persuasion above compulsion, gives to man a higher status than that of a merely "dominant species." To be "dominant" in a biological sense would mean only that man has the power to use all species beneath him as means, as for example, eating them, incorporating them bodily into himself. This is no very great status of dignity, for it was once probably occupied by the great cats. It is not then in superior activity as such, being always the predator and almost never the prey, but in the direction of that activity. If this is a valid deduction then the dignity of man does not rest in man's superior reason, where reason is clever induction and deduction, the knowhow of problem-solving, which is often argued as the human title to superiority. Rather, the argument of Whitehead defends the tradition of man as rational "a little lower than the angels." This reason is clearly differentiated from mere intellect when, in *The Function of Reason*, Whitehead makes the point of human ambiguity: man shares his reason with the foxes and also with the gods.

Although Whitehead neglected ethics, he nevertheless sees man in the situation of any organism, that is, not only dependent upon other organisms, but destroying them so that he might live. If so, then all organisms are in a situation that is "moral." An organism requires food. "The living society may, or may not, be a higher type of organism than the food which it disintegrates. But whether or not it be for the general good, life is robbery. It is at this point that with life morals become acute. The robber requires justification" (*PR*, 160). The passages break off to consider whether "God" can be invoked to solve the problem, as did theistic Victorians, who argued that man had been given all other animals for himself. Obviously Whitehead does not have a divinely constituted hierarchy in which man has the prerogatives of lordship over all beasts, birds, serpents, and fish. Whitehead's God is not a Creator or a Preserver, and there are for God's primordial envisagement no particulars to be concerned with (*PR*, 160). The moral problem is then man's, to be solved in relationship to nature's other organisms. If life is a robbery that requires justification, what is this justification? If unjustified, can there be atonement for wrong? In more modern terms than sin, if man destroys individuals and even other species wholesale, can he make restitution?

The answer implicit in the conclusion of *Science and the Modern World* is that the human species, apparently alone, is capable of knowing its responsibility to every other species and to accept responsibility for nature as a whole. Hence we go to Whitehead's "Requisites for Social Progress" to examine his ecological philosophy.

Human Responsibility for the Order of Nature

The "Philosophy of Organism" because of the conception of all forms of life as interdependent is a philosophy that can be applied in ecology. A generation before this new study of man in the environment had emerged, Whitehead had expressed dissatisfaction with the sharp dualism postulated by Descartes between mind and matter that alienated man from his physical environment. "The effect of this sharp division between nature and life has poisoned all subsequent philosophy. Even when the coordinate existence of the two types of actualities is abandoned, there is no proper fusion of the two in most modern schools of thought. For some, nature is mere appearance and mind is the sole reality. For others, physical nature is the sole reality and mind is an epiphenomenon. Here the phrases 'mere appearance' and 'epiphenomenon' obviously carry the implication of slight importance for the understanding of the final nature of things" (*MT*, 204–5).

What is so unfortunate about such a philosophy of mind and matter? "It omits the lower forms of life, such as vegetation and the lower animal types. These forms touch upon human mentality at their highest, and upon inorganic nature at their lowest" (*MT*, 204).

Whereas the dualism of Descartes "lead[s] straight to the theory of a materialistic, mechanistic nature, surveyed by cogitating minds," organicism presents a "systematic totality . . . as one complex of things." There is no sharp division between "nature as an interplay of bodies, colors, sounds, scents, tastes and touches and other various bodily feelings, displayed as in space, in patterns of mutual separation by intervening volumes, and of individual shape" (*SMW*, 209).

Rather than a private world of experience and a private world of morals, based on the "bare valuelessness of mere matter," organicism implies "reverence in the treatment of natural or artistic beauty." Organicism draws from the "true relation of each organism to its environment" the implication of "the intrinsic worth of the environment which must be allowed its weight in any consideration of final ends." (*SMW*, 281–82, turning negations of mechanism into affirmations of organicism.)

Whitehead's analysis links the values of artistic to those of natural beauty. He defines art as the "habit of enjoying vivid values" and he finds "an appreciation of the infinite variety of vivid values achieved by an organism in its proper environment" (*SMW*, 287, 286). It is significant that in "Requisites for Social Progress" he has no specific case of value from painting, sculpture, architecture, music, dance, but several specific protests against the degradation of the environment. The tragic side of industrialization was contempt for beauty. "A striking example of this state of mind in the middle of the nineteenth century is to be seen in London where the marvelous beauty of the estuary of the Thames, as it curves through the city, is wantonly defaced by the Charing Cross railway bridge, constructed apart from any reference to aesthetic values" (*SMW*, 281).

Apart from the reverence for beauty, in the context of moral concern for an intrinsic good for people generally, the philosophy of organicism demands inclusion of the beauty experienced by the poet. Whitehead recognizes more than "scientific materialism" to be corrected: there are also the "aesthetic errors of Protestantism . . . , the natural greed of mankind, . . . the abstractions of political economy." Robert Southey "found out a way, he tells us, in which the effects of manufactures and agriculture may be compared. And what is this way?" asks Macaulay in reviewing *Colloquies on Society.* "To stand on a hill, to look at a cottage and a factory, and to see which is the prettier" (*SMW*, 292–93). To mock Southey, in Whitehead's analysis, was to ignore "the evils of the early industrial system," which all now acknowledge.

The philosophy of organicism is based on correcting the metaphysics that holds "that matter in motion is the one concrete validity in nature." The implication of materialism is that "aesthetic values form an adventitious, irrelevant addition," and then moral values can be ignored if one regards man as an animal in nature (*SMW*, 293).

The evolutionary ethic of the post-Darwinian era, sometimes called "social Darwinism," is clearly the target of Whitehead's finest statement of an environmental ethic. It is perhaps his finest claim to be considered a moral philosopher, if not a technical ethicist. The position is that a better science as well as a better ethic can be based on the organicist metaphysics that recognizes the interdependence of living forms. The concept arrived at is clearly that of the ecosystem.

Between animals there is cooperation, not merely competition. The philosophy of organism accordingly redresses the balance and stresses the success of organisms in modifying their environments. Different species depend upon one another and together help to maintain the environment. The examples of Whitehead are drawn from human populations, such as Indians in North America, microbes in the Brazilian forests, and the dependence of animal life upon sexual differentiation. It is cooperation that marks the most successful, and the animals that illustrate the antagonism of force tend to be less successful. Thus Whitehead rejects such a gross exaggeration and falsehood as "the Gospel of Force," which probably includes Nietzsche's version, the "Will to Power."

The justification of the robbery of eating can then be only that by so doing, more life is created. But the atonement, man reconciled with the whole of life, must also be the creation of a higher level of life. The whole ethical position may be characterized as "naturalistic," provided certain value principles are accepted. Life is, on the whole, better than death. Intensity is, on the whole, better than dullness and boredom. Harmony is, on the whole, better than strife. And how are we to know whether these are true? No authority is offered other than direct inspection of nature. It is appropriate to say that the ethics is on an aesthetic basis, yet there is an irreducible moral question of justification, so that it is not quite right to call the position ethical aestheticism. The appeal to the compatibility of intensity with harmony is, in Whitehead, best argued on the basis of civilization, the subject of the next chapter.

Order-Disorder: Concluding Amplified Theory of Cosmos

We began our search for order in experience with the initial encounter with the untidy, ragged world. Does Whitehead think that science has given us that tidy rationality in which all events are governed by law? Does he think that from the sciences he can defend a perfect order of nature? If the mathematical conception of this order of nature rests on the continuities of space and time, then the evidence of recent physics forced Whitehead to modify this conception.

Because we included his belief in cosmos, as we found him rejecting any miracle that a train could go from one station to another by a leap taking no time, the shock was that physics discovered that energy comes in discrete pulses that will be here, then there, but not in between. In *Science and the Modern World* Whitehead includes a chapter on "Quantum Theory," a subject of vast interest in the philosophy of science. What is Whitehead's solution?

If belief in the order of nature were based on the perfectly continuous motion of all bodies in space and time, then it would be now refuted by the physics of electrons. The theory is that "an electron does not continuously traverse its path in space. . . . It appears at a series of discrete positions in space which it occupies for successive durations of time" (*SMW*, 52).

The illustrations given by analogy would indeed indicate a highly disorderly nature, even one of miraculous leaps. "It is as though an automobile moving at the average rate of thirty miles an hour along a road . . . appeared successively at the successive milestones, remaining two minutes at each milestone" (*SMW*, 52). If electrons have "the character which some people have assigned to the Mahatmas of Tibet," then "we have to revise all our notions of the ultimate character of material existence" (*SMW*, 53).

The philosophy of organism is, because of the paramount importance of temporal process, able to "conceive each primordial element as a vibratory ebb and flow of an underlying energy, or activity" (*SMW*, 53). Then the "element" is no longer an atom or an aspect of an atom but an "organized system of vibratory streaming of energy" (*SMW*, 53). Then, at any instant, an element is like a wave, "nothing at any instant" (*SMW*, 54). Therefore there is no answer to where the electron is at any moment, and the only answer is "its average position at the center of each period."

Whitehead adds that "energy" itself is an abstraction, and to deal with such an abstraction in quantitative terms is but another instance of "the doctrine of old Pythagoras" (*SMW*, 55).

The philosophy of organism is also able to redefine "order" to allow that "an orbit of an electron can be . . . a series of detached positions, and not . . . a continuous line" (*SMW*, 196). This can be secured by conceiving "continuity of the complex of events [as derivative] from the relationships of extensiveness; whereas the temporality arises from the realization in a subject-event of a pattern which requires for its display that the whole of a duration be spatialized (i.e. arrested), as given by its aspects of the event. Thus realization proceeds *via* a succession of epochal durations; and the continuous transition, i.e., the organic deformation, is within the duration which is already given" (*SMW*, 196–97).

Then the diagram of the orbit of an electron would be "exhibited by a series of detached dots" (*SMW*, 197). What is represented by a dot? Whitehead calls "any organism of the primary genus a primate" and adds "there may be different species of primates" (*SMW*, 191),

Just as space and time were defined as relations between events, so now, following relativity, "the relative motion of two primates means simply that their organic patterns are utilizing diverse space-time systems. If two primates do not continue either mutually at rest, or mutually in uniform relative motion, at least one of them is changing its intrinsic space-time system" (*SMW*, 192).

Not only are there changes in the very space-time systems, but also the patterns themselves may change. "The pattern may be essentially one of aesthetic contrasts requiring a lapse of time for its unfolding. A tune is an example of such a pattern." This succession of contrasts makes endurance into "reiteration" (*SMW*, 193).

The inclusion of quantum theory in a general cosmology is extended in *Process and Reality*. Whereas earlier the quantum is defined in terms of organism, here the quantum is the fundamental unit. "I shall use the term 'event' in the more general sense of a nexus of actual occasions, inter-related in some determinate fashion in one extensive quantum" (*PR*, 113). We have yet to examine the later metaphysical system with the technical notion of "nexus of actual occasions," which must remain undefined. The point is that the quantum called for reconsideration of the order of nature.

Formerly the order of nature had excluded discontinuity. The philoso-phy of organism can accept discontinuities on the level of higher complex organisms such as man. Ordinary language has led us to overlook the discontinuities and to smooth out change into regularity.

Just as these quanta of energy are vibratory, and what we know is their rhythmic periods, so we can know this of ourselves.

It is said that "men are rational." This is palpably false: they are only intermit-tently rational—merely liable to rationality. Again the phrase "Socrates is mortal" is only another way of saying that "perhaps he will die." The intellect of Socrates is intermittent: he occasionally sleeps and he can be drugged or stunned. (*PR*, 122)

If our concept of the order of nature is also tied to "enduring substances sustaining persistent qualities, either essentially or accidentally," then we are asked to abandon these common sense notions except for practical purposes (*PR*, 122). The older metaphysics had no place for real change, and "a monistic universe [reduced change to] the illusion of change." An organistic cosmology is of "a pluralistic universe in which 'change' means the diversities among the actual entities which belong to some one society of a definite type" (*PR*, 122–23).

The fundamental question is: why are there different kinds of things? The "modern quantum theory [presents] the dissolution of quanta into vibrations. . . ." Although Newton would have been surprised, Plato would have felt his *Timaeus* supported, for he

accounted for the sharp-cut differences between kinds of natural things, by assuming an approximation of the molecules to the fundamental kinds respec-tively to the mathematical forms of the regular solids. He also assumed that certain qualitative contrasts in occurrences, such as that between musical notes,

depended on the participation of these occurrences in some of the simpler ratios
between integral numbers. He thus obtained a reason why there should be an
approximation to sharp-cut differences between kinds of molecules and why
there should be sharp-cut relations of harmony standing out amid dissonance.
(*PR*, 145)

Thus a Pythagorean conception of cosmos is reformulated with a
doctrine of harmony and contrast. The "differences" are sharp-cut, but are
not logically incompatible. There is an hierarchical ordering, with "higher
contrasts depend[ent] on the assemblage of a multiplicity of lower contrasts . . ." (*PR*, 145).

Quantum theory then is but "the latest instance of a well-marked
character of nature. . . ." One example is "the sharply distinguished
genera and species which we find in nature. There might be an occasional
bunching of individuals round certain typical forms. . . ." Whitehead's
Pythagorean cosmos has an explanation for "the almost complete absence
of intermediate forms," as it does of the forms of atoms, which are the
"limited number of ways in which atoms can be combined so as to form
molecules." These aspects of nature, studied in biology and chemistry,
have been in the past "only explained by some *ad hoc* dogmatic assumption" (*PR*, 145).

If there is an eternal realm of distinguishable forms, and our world is the
actualization of these forms, then nature would be expected only to exhibit
distinctions. This seems to restate the argument essentially. Since the
realm of eternal objects is the vision of the primordial nature of God, only
so interpreted would it follow that "the quantum is that standpoint in the
extensive continuum which is consonant with the subjective aim in its
original derivation from God. Here 'God' is that actuality in the world, in
virtue of which there is physical 'law.'" And only if the quantum were
ultimately like a "number" of Pythagorean cosmology would it make sense
to talk of "the actualization of the quantum *in solido*" (*PR*, 434).

Nature is marked by different tendencies called "adversion" and "aver-
sion," turning toward and turning away. There can be transmission of
energy or its attenuation or elimination. An organism then can be conceived as "the summation of the forms of energy which flow in upon it in
all their multiplicity of detail. It receives, and it transmits. . . ." Transmission is "from individual actuality to individual actuality. Thus some
sort of quantum-theory in physics, relevant to the existing type of cosmic
order, is to be expected." It is then crucial to formulate a metaphysics with
categories that imply this transmission (*PR*, 389).

The fundamental importance of Whitehead's revival of Pythagoreanism for the belief in order comes in the form of a revival of the myth of Plato's *Timaeus*. Rather than beginning with divine order, as in the biblical view of the almighty Creator, there is "an aboriginal disorder, chaotic according to our ideals." Rather than "a wholly transcendent God creating out of nothing an accidental universe," there is the evolution of "the present cosmic epoch." Rather than holding that the universe with its type of order "came into being, and will pass out of being, according to the fiat of Jehovah," there is "the evolution of a new type of order based on new types of dominant societies" (*PR,* 146).

Although our metaphysical imagination has been dominated by the biblical belief in Jehovah, there is the Platonic view of this aboriginal disorder. Whitehead, as ever when there is a particularly crucial point, appeals to poetry. In this case he quotes Milton's *Paradise Lost,* Book 2:

> The secrets of the hoary deep, a dark
> Illimitable ocean, without bound,
> Without dimension, where length, breadth and highth,
> And time and place are lost; where eldest night
> and Chaos, ancestors of Nature, hold
> Eternal anarchy amidst the noise
> Of endless wars, and by confusion stand.

The passage is, of course, dependent on Hesiod, whose vision of earth begins with chaos and night and then comes broad-breasted earth. One way of saying that there is a "real potentiality" which takes on form in becoming actual, is now common among scientists who refer to a primeval "soup." Whitehead might have appealed to this had he written a generation later. But he uses the image from Milton of "Satan's journey [which] helped to evolve order; for he left a permanent track, useful for the devils and damned" (*PR,* 146–47).

The new conception is not an atheism content to affirm only the eternity of "the material universe, with its present type of order . . ." (*PR,* 146). Many had limited the alternatives to Genesis or some version of the materialism of Democritus and Lucretius. What Whitehead does on the basis of his philosophy of organism is to reconceive divine creation. The process of the actual world is a "real incoming of forms into real potentiality, issuing into that real togetherness which is an actual thing." The creation of the world is the incoming of a type of order establishing a cosmic epoch (*PR,* 147).

Chapter Five

The Harmony of Civilization: Man's Search for a New Order

The Problem of Civilization

There is a continuity of levels, and beginning from the rock, Whitehead's traditional example of the relatively lifeless, we rise through plants and animals to the human level of society. We have seen that human life is dependent upon an environment. In considering the emergence of civilized life, the same principle of evolution is illustrated in the emergence of tribes, nations, empires, in succession, together with religions of ever-widening scope. When the time span is of the order of six thousand years, there can be observed some clear evidence of progress. We should expect a principle of order, the correlation of the sequence of temporal emergence with the sequence of higher types of relations between persons. Whitehead, faced with the choice between the more optimistic belief in "the steady march toward perfection" and "organization on the whole . . . throughout the world by slow and interrupted steps," rejected the more optimistic view, that of Herbert Spencer, and preferred the less optimistic view, that of Charles Darwin. The opening statement of *Science and the Modern World* is the theme also of *Religion in the Making* and *Adventures of Ideas:* "the progress of civilization is not wholly a uniform drift towards better things" (*SMW,* 1).

Can we judge the value of a person or a society of persons by survival? Here is the difference between the organism and its environment, and this difference is most pronounced on the human level: the attainment of "independence of individuality with self interests," or in short, "the emergence of life [is] a bid for freedom" (*S,* 64–65). The stone has little freedom but endures. A person has freedom but perishes. The sacrifice of length of life is gain in idiosyncrasy and thereby the heterogeneous scope of possibilities open to us. Because of the dangers of disorganization, human society must be stabilized by many bonds, such as love of country and a common language and literature, without which we cannot maintain a nation (*S,* 68).

Can we have both order and freedom in civilization? When freedom means unlimited choice for the individual, the order of obligations seems contrary, and we might conclude that the more freedom, the less order, and that we must sacrifice one to gain the other. Without tracing the detailed steps by which Whitehead illustrates his norm, freedom is not primarily freedom from constraint, but freedom to accomplish positive goals, such as the production of responsible institutions, the arts and the sciences. "The essence of freedom is the practicability of purpose" (*AI,* 84).

What Whitehead's philosophy of civilization does is to define goals of a most general sort which are to bring about a "close interaction of individuals." Thus "society" is defined (*S,* 64). Although the account begins in biological nature, the philosophy is teleological, and the emphasis is upon the goals. There are conservative ideologies that stress continuity of custom, such as Edmund Burke's. Whitehead agrees with this as ensuring order, yet not with the implication drawn, that society can survive only by "the negation of progressive reform" (*S,* 73). His dominant stress is liberal, on the maximizing of freedom of each individual.

We shall sketch the theory of "Progress and Freedom" and "Progress and Order," in the next two sections, to prepare for the fourth section, "Harmony," and conclude with "Harmony and Strife."

Progress and Freedom

Exactly what does Whitehead mean when he writes that "the progress of civilization is not wholly a uniform drift towards better things" (*SMW,* 1)? One meaning is based on the relation between science and philosophy we have already seen. This is that the progress of physical science implied the decline of philosophy. The reason is that physical science was so closely tied to materialistic mechanism that forced philosophy into body-mind dualism. If nature is nothing but atoms in motion, then all value must be subjective or in the mind, and therefore existence is meaningless, and philosophy is "ruined" (*SMW,* 82). Another meaning is based on the relation between modern civilization and religion. The same periods that evidence the most spectacular successes in the sciences are also the centuries during which religious institutions are weakened and religious thought enfeebled. Although there were fervent humanitarian religious leaders in the eighteenth century, and Whitehead admired John Wesley and John Woolman particularly, it was as applying old ideals rather than advancing new theories to watch those of the sciences (*SMW*, Ch. 12). A vacuum was left by doctrines of "the mechanism of matter," and there came the poets of the "Romantic Reaction" to show us the importance of art to excite us by vivid expression of emotion (*SMW*, Chs. 5, 13).

Whitehead selected one great ideal which promoted "the slow drift of mankind towards civilization" (*AI*, vii). This is the ideal of the freedom of every individual person. In ancient times, when civilization was based upon slavery, it was novel for the prophets of Israel to protest against "compulsory degradation." The moral judgment of Jews and Christians that each soul was of worth has become the modern doctrine that there are "essential rights." The kindliness of individual slave owners only palliates a wicked institution and eases our conscience as we participate in iniquity (*AI*, 16–17).

The ancients presupposed inequality as the moderns presuppose equality of persons. Yet both situations are ambiguous. Slave owners were embarrassed by "the plain facts of moral feeling." Now egalitarians find their theory difficult to reconcile with "another group of plain facts, perplexing, irreconcilable only to be conceived as a hateful brute necessity" (*AI*, 15). Whitehead here leaves us to consider the inequalities of talent, effort, and achievement, and the necessities of hierarchical organization.

The roots in ancient cultures of our modern enfranchisement progressively bear fruit of humanitarian concern for the disadvantaged and oppressed. Not only fervent Jewish prophets, but also Greek philosophers, with an ideal of the human soul, and Roman lawyers, with judgments of what is naturally and universally right, contributed essentially to Christianity. It was never carried into an actual Kingdom of God, but "God has been a great resource: a lot of things, which won't work on earth, can be conceived as true in his sight" (*AI*, 15).

The fruits of the "essential greatness of the human soul" come when the revolutionaries clarify, broaden, and apply the idea. The French *philosophes* build upon the "alliance of philosophy, law, and religion" (*AI*, 23). The ideas themselves had been, since Plato's Academy, the Stoic lawyers, and the Christian Gospels, in circulation for over two thousand years (*AI*, 24). We see then why Whitehead talks of "drift." Progress comes very slowly.

The conservative will find Whitehead too radical. And the radical will find him too conservative. It is not lack of sympathy with the oppressed that leads Whitehead to appreciate the necessity of strong institutions.

His defense of custom, traditions, and moderation in policy is based on an appreciation of order.

We began by defining progress as the achievement of freedom. But there is a necessary complementary truth: "civilization is the maintenance of social order." Only within an order can there be "the victory of persuasion over force" (*AI*, 105).

Progress and Order

Exactly why does Whitehead identify progress with social order? The freedom that Whitehead intended was not only the freedom of inalienable rights, but also what is called positive freedom, the rational pursuit of the good. Whitehead does not hold the model of the state as an organism in which each limb is coordinated to serve the whole body, particularly not the idealistic model of each class observing its place in a hierarchy. But there is in the ideal society the harmonization of all efforts. It is often pointed out that there is a meaning of freedom common in Anglo-American life since Locke that the individual is free when there is no constraint or limitation upon his thought and action. The other meaning is that freedom is achieved direction and pursuit of reason and the good, and some say God, as in the Book of Common Prayer, deep in Whitehead's consciousness, "God, whose service is perfect freedom."

Whitehead is Platonic in the sense of basing society on reason's direct apprehension of the Good: ". . . the soul freely conform[s] its nature to the supremacy of insight. It is the reconciliation of freedom with the compulsion of the truth. In this sense the captive can be free, taking as his own the supreme insight, the indwelling persuasions towards the harmony which is the height of existence" (*AI*, 86).

The apprehension of the Good is the absorption of the changeless in changing circumstances, and the freedom springs directly "from the source of all harmony" (*AI*, 86). This service of God would be slavery if devoted to the nation or to a social class. It is not God in the sense of power that compels but of harmony that persuades rationally. The other way of stating this apprehension is that it is of a divine order, said to be the "reason why the universe should not be steadily relapsing into lawless chaos" (*AI*, 147).

Often in the nineteenth century the idea of progress took the place of utopia and even was a surrogate for God. One expression from Alfred, Lord Tennyson viewed progress as producing perfect order: "that far-off divine event to which the whole creation moves" (*PR*, 169). Whitehead rejects the conception of history as a series with a final term. It is fallacious to think that "all types of seriality necessarily involve terminal instances" (*PR*, 169). It is furthermore false to think of any one state of order as perfect, beyond which there can be no better state. The myth of utopia then goes the way of the mistake of thinking that there can be such a thing as the greatest number.

The redefinition of "order," made possible by the logic of relations, allows a rethinking of the famous nineteenth century watch word "progress and order." What are Whitehead's most distinctive claims that make his theory an advance beyond familiar, and now rejected, theories of the same name?

There is no one order, but many orders. Whitehead finds this true both in nature and in society because there are as many series discoverable in events as there are factors in the facts. "The" order is always ambiguous, even though we commonly assume that magnitude is "the" order of the integers, as in 1, 2, 3, etc. But suppose we draw these numbers from a hat, as in a lottery. Then "the" significant order is the time order of drawing, and 3 might be first and win the prize (*ESP*, 197). So in society, we have specialized functions. We have made progress by becoming specialized and more professional. But this kind of progress means lack of balance, and the vision whereby the whole can be coordinated. "The progressiveness in detail only adds to the danger produced by the feebleness of coordination" (*SMW*, 283).

"Order" is not necessarily good, nor is "disorder" bad. Why has past thought identified the orderly as good in contrast to bad disorder? Because our ancestors thought only of design, and the last term of the series was the desired goal. But there may be, argues the skeptic Philo in Hume's *Dialogues*, a sequence of steps in the process of madness or of decay.[1] By defining "order" as a relation that is asymmetrical, transitive, and connected, we have a purely analytic and descriptive concept that begs no question of value. In considering dimensions of civilized value, Whitehead does not overlook steps that are not ideal, such as developing "finer imagination," but merely instrumental. Science advanced in the nineteenth century because there were German opticians who manufactured superior instruments (*SMW*, 166–67). This analysis allows us to specify the standard of evaluation.

When we judge progress, we need always to specify the scale of time. All we can ever consider is a limited subset of an infinite sequence. Whitehead reminds us that "the present type of order in the world has arisen from an unimaginable past, and . . . will find its grave in an unimaginable future" (*RM,* 160). It follows that we can have no truth about progress of the whole of cosmic or even of human history. Whether the subset is a case of progress depends necessarily then, among other conditions, on whether we take a decade, century, or millennium. Whitehead is always careful to specify that it is the nineteenth century, for example, that with parliamentary government and industrial expansion, scholarship could be organized so that "progress did not have to wait for the occasional genius, or the occasional lucky thought" (*SMW,* 142). But progress of the past four centuries makes the whole modern period depend upon the geniuses of the seventeenth century.

Judgments of progress depend upon empirical knowledge of diverse areas of culture. One area may progress while another retrogresses. Hence, the question "does the nineteenth century show progress" depends upon whether one judges its products, for example, aesthetically. With industrial progress, Whitehead agrees with the poets that it shows artistic decline.

Because of the empirical reference and conceptual discrimination, Whitehead diverges from such a radical ideology as Marx's or such a conservative ideology as Burke's. Marx presents the contrast between philosophies that "have only *interpreted* the world, in various ways" and philosophies aiming *"to change it."*[2] Whitehead's progress is both a theory guiding "the composition of historical narrative" and also "the driving force of ideas in history" (*AI,* 5). On the conservative side, Whitehead warns against the abstract dreams of "paper plans for society. . . . Successful progress creeps from point to point, testing each step" (*AI,* 24).

Harmony

Harmony can be thought in two very different ways. One is the regularity discovered in the movement of the planets. The other is in the beauty created by artists. There is harmony discovered in the cosmos and harmony created by humans. We have already seen that Whitehead ascribes the first to an "iron necessity [but the latter to] the aesthetic harmony that stands before [the universe] as a living ideal moulding the general flux in its broken progress towards finer subtler issues" (*SMW,* 28). The way in which this aesthetic harmony is itself there in the cosmos apart from man is part of Whitehead's metaphysics, especially the doctrine of God. Although "harmony" has many meanings, the classic four of Pythagoreans include an ideal of soceity.

Harmos is ancient Greek for "joint" and Galen meant by "harmony" the union of our bodily limbs. Most of us think in music, as did the Pythagoreans, that harmony is the "agreement or concord of sounds." In the modern world it came to mean not only the relation between classes in a state, but also the toleration of diverse religions.[3]

Harmony became a powerful intellectual tool because of "the interweaving of qualitative fact with geometrical and quantitative composition" (*AI*, 191). By this Whitehead means that the beautiful sounds depend upon the length of the strings, and that the same necessity of proper proportion holds in architecture. Thus the qualitative depends upon the quantitative. Plato's cosmology rested on "an intense belief that a knowledge of mathematical relations would prove the key to unlock the mysteries of relatedness within Nature . . ." (*AI*, 194). Whitehead considers the Platonic doctrine to be superior to the Aristotelian and that modern science has drastically reduced the importance of Aristotelian classification based on qualitative predicates. The Platonic logic asks "How much?" "In what proportion?" and the significance is easily grasped. Proportion makes all the difference between CO which "will kill you, when CO_2 will only give you a headache. Also CO_2 is a necessary element for the dilution of oxygen in the atmosphere; but too much or too little is equally harmful" (*AI*, 196).

There are not only kinds of harmony, such as these proportions in chemical compounds and mixtures, as well as harmony in the achievements of art, but also applications in human relations. To these is applied, as to cases of beauty, the distinction between minor and major. Minor harmony "is the absence of mutual inhibition" (*AI*, 324). Major harmony is not the mere absence of discord, but a synthesis of contrasts. Major harmony is "strong" in the senses of "variety of detail with effective contrast, which is Massiveness, and Intensity Proper which is comparative magnitude . . ." (*AI*, 325).

What now is meant by progress in civilization? "Nothing other than the unremitting aim at the major perfections of harmony" (*AI*, 349). Should a society aim at minor harmony, in which it may well succeed, or at major harmony, in which it will surely fail? The standard requires the latter. "Progress is founded upon the experience of discordant feelings. The social value of liberty lies in its production of discords" (*AI*, 330).

The contrast between minor harmony and major harmony is that between peace and adventure. Peace, as absence of war, is a great good, but adventure, striving for novel excellence, is better. The minor harmonies are illustrated from Hellenism, which in all aspects of civilization became imitative, repetitive, conventional, and in Whitehead's evaluation "stale" (*AI*, 331). The contrasting greatness came from new religions, such as Christianity, and new peoples, the barbarians. What did the new religion of the new people produce? A strong individuality, an attention to detail worthy of value in itself, is evident in the Gothic cathedral. What is meant by intensity of contrast is evident in Chartres Cathedral. "Each detail claims a permanent existence for its own sake, and then surrenders it for the sake of the whole composition" (*AI*, 364).

The Platonic "Harmony of Harmonies" is the norm of Truth, Beauty, and Goodness. Truth "is the conformation of Appearance to Reality." This is limited, as contrasted to Beauty, and is valuable because it may serve other ends. Beauty is self-justifying (*AI*, 341–42). There is a "Truth of feeling" that is Beauty, even "a Truth of Supreme Beauty" (*AI*, 343). This kind of Beauty is good, and discloses "a sense of rightness in the deepest Harmony" (*AI*, 343–44). Not that this norm is intended by Whitehead to force art into serving moral goodness, but that the real world can be disclosed as beautiful, and therefore as good (*AI*, 345). This step is necessary to justify a theory of God.

Whitehead reformulates the traditional Truth, Beauty, and Goodness of the Platonic tradition. The new "Harmony of Harmonies" is called "Peace," and this "calms destructive turbulence and completes civilization" (*AI*, 367). "Thus a society is to be termed civilized whose members participate in the five qualities - Truth, Beauty, Adventure, Art, Peace" (*AI*, 367).

All actual attainment in history is particular, and therefore gained by exclusion of "the unbounded welter of contrary possibilites" (*AI*, 356). Evil comes in history when diverse groups of idealists attempt to actualize incompatible ideals (*AI*, 357).

But what are all the ideals together, which may be achieved in sequence, if not conjointly? These are aspects of the vision of God. "We must conceive the Divine Eros as the active entertainment of all ideals, with the urge to their finite realization, each in its due season. Thus a process must be inherent in God's nature, whereby his infinity is acquiring realization" (*AI*, 357).

Harmony and Strife

Harmony has been neglected in Western thought since Leibniz made great use of it in his system. Rather than going back to the Pythagoreans and Plato, as did Whitehead, to grasp what we have called "the Pythago-rean vision," critics considered only the bland optimism of Leibniz, that all happens for the best. This doctrine is no less false and offensive to Whitehead than to Voltaire. Because the industrial revolution was secured through highly competitive means, there were many who did not even respect harmony as an ideal, even if unachievable in civilization, but rather exalted strife. In spite of his hatred of the nineteenth-century bourgeoisie, the best-known philosopher of strife is Friedrich Nietzsche.

What the notions of "form" and "harmony" were to Plato, that the notions of "individuality" and "competition" were to the nineteenth century. God had placed his bow in the skies as a symbol; and the strip of colors, rightly read, spelt "competition." The prize to be competed for was "life." Unsuccessful competi-tors died; and thus, by a beautiful provision of nature, ceased from constituting a social problem.

Now it is quite obvious that a much needed corrective to an unqualified, sentimental humanitarianism is here being supplied. Strife is at least as real a fact in the world as Harmony. If you side with Francis Bacon and concentrate on the efficient causes, you can interpret large features of the growth of structure in terms of "strife." If, with Plato, you fix attention on the end, rationally worthy, you can interpret large features in terms of "harmony." But until some outline of understanding has been reached which elucidates the interfusion of strife and harmony, the intellectual driving force of successive generations will sway uneasily between the two (*AI,* 39–40).

Whitehead grants that in much recent history strife was fundamental and "harmony was a secondary effect, merely Romance gilding Strife" (*AI,* 40).

What of the reconciliation of Strife with Harmony?

The political, liberal faith of the nineteenth century was a compromise between the individualistic, competitive doctrine of strife and the optimistic doctrine of harmony. It was believed that the laws of the Universe were such that the strife of individuals issued in the progressive realization of a harmonious society. In this way, it was possible to cherish the emotional belief in the Brotherhood of Man, while engaging in relentless competition with all individual men. (*AI,* 41)

There is no logical contradiction in the theory of liberalism. The repug-nancy is between the misery of workers in factory and mine, when competition is unregulated, and the profession of humanitarian faith.

The philosophy of organism is a synthesis of order and progress. It does not reject change with novelty, but aims to include disorderly elements in the basic ongoing living order. Such a philosophy of civilization carries with it the promise of new orders without end. The basis of such a philosophy must lie in the character of the universe. To the order of the system we proceed.

Chapter Six

Speculative Philosophy: The Order of a System

A Scheme of General Ideas

Every phase of Whitehead's philosophy shows a deep concern with some mode of order. His account of life and learning demonstrates the dialectical struggle between opposites and toward the harmony of synthesis. The work in mathematics and logic was to demonstrate their underlying unity and as sciences of order, giving a fresh and applicable definition of "series." Such linear orders are illustrated in the dimensions of space and time, and underlie the grasp of regularities in nature. Our prehension of processes gives us an underlying comprehension of human persons as organisms of high grade responsible for the lower organisms without whom they cannot live and for whom they are responsible. Although the philosophy of organism recognized the natural hierarchy in which man finds himself at the top, civilization is defined as the effort to secure equality among persons cooperating harmoniously. Perhaps all along there had been the assumption of an ultimate ground of unity in multiplicity, some ultimate bond of being. Yet the studies prior to *Science and the Modern World* and *Religion in the Making* had seemed those of a mathematician and a philosopher of science, and readers were taken by surprise when one of the topics was "God," and various embarrassed explanations appeared.

Whitehead's motivation, set forth in the "Preface" to *Process and Reality,* is a defense of metaphysics in the historic sense of a system of general ideas. The scheme must be "adequate for the interpretation of the ideas and problems which form the complex texture of civilized thought." *Religion in the Making* goes a step further in meaning by "metaphysics" the "science which seeks to discover the general ideas which are indispensably relevant to the analysis of everything that happens" (*RM,* 84 ft. does not define "science," but obviously it is in a much broader sense than either inductive or deductive, and is probably defined as "a true understanding of the cosmos," in which "true" bears all the meanings Whitehead details in *Religion in the Making,* but best outlined below as coherent, logical, necessary and adequate). To be intelligible the scheme must demonstrate its power "to put the various elements of our experience into a consistent relation to each other." We have already seen the philosophy of organism applied to area after area of experience in an endeavor to be "complete" (*PR,* v). Whitehead's way of interpreting past philosophers was to use their divergences to correct the one-sidedness and "inconsistent presuppositions underlying their inherited modes of expression." The fault of a "system" is characteristically to abandon ideas that do not easily fit, even when they appeal to experience. The philosophy of organism intends to achieve a "complete cosmology, . . . a system of ideas which brings the aesthetic, moral, and religious interests into relation with those concepts of the world which have their origin in natural science" (*PR,* vi).

Although the title *Process and Reality* harks back to "the reality is the process," which we quoted from *Science and the Modern World,* and seems to be a philosophy of flux, as in Heraclitus and Bergson, it is better to study the scheme as an independent system based on the study of orders in all the areas of life. Whitehead was concerned with "permanances amid the inescapable flux," and those who cite only Heraclitus as an ancestor ignore "the complete problem of metaphysics," which is the problem of balance between the two (*PR,* 318). There is indeed a Heraclitean moment in the philosophy of organism, but it is in tension with a Pythagorean moment. Less cryptically, the flux is read in mathematical terms. There is not only an undifferentiated flow but differentiation into units capable of orderly statement. "Mathematical physics translates the saying of Heraclitus, 'All things flow,' into its own language. It then becomes, All things are vectors. Mathematical physics also accepts the atomistic doctrine of Democritus. It translates it into the phrase, All flow of energy obeys 'quantum' conditions" (*PR,* 471).

Among strong beliefs are these: that philosophy ought in our age to become once again systematic, and the true method is to follow one's ideas rigorously to their conclusions. Even if one does not acknowledge any metaphysical beliefs, much less a system, there still are metaphysical presuppositions that control us. One can develop a system without claiming that it is beyond doubt, indeed acknowledging that it will be corrected.

The defense of system under these four heads of timeliness, applicability, inevitability, and tentativeness is given in response to those who have claimed that metaphysics is out of date and archaic, idle and fruitless, avoidable as distracting from particular topics, and dogmatic and doctrinaire. Without citing the antimetaphysical opinions which have dominated in the late nineteenth and twentieth centuries, the position is defended. Rather than reject all systems because Hegel's was arrogant, Whitehead's solution is to develop a scheme of ideas that does not claim to be final and complete. Actually, he argues that scientific thought is itself dominated by unacknowledged concepts. Therefore it is simple honesty to make categories explicit, and good method to follow all the consequences. The great caveat is to avoid dogmatism, and to encourage criticism.

There remains the final reflection, how shallow, puny, and imperfect are efforts to sound the depths in the nature of things. In philosophical discussion, the merest hint of dogmatic certainty as to finality of statement is an exhibition of folly. (PR, x)

Metaphysics is called "speculative philosophy" not because it is risky as a gamble, but because it is concerned with seeing the whole, as from a watchtower. This is the wider subject than even "cosmology," which occurs in the title and as the introduction to the last chapter (PR, 518).

Every term in the definition is then explicated. Among the salient differences from previous systems is the inclusion of things enjoyed and willed, as well as perceived and thought. This is to avoid the rebuke that the system is a "bloodless dance of categories." The categories are related organically so that "in isolation they are meaningless." Logic forbids contradiction, but such a logical concept must itself be interpreted within the system. But the system, though "coherent" and "logical," is not purely rational. "Applicable" and "adequate" express its empirical side. The "necessity" is then not from deduction but from "universality throughout all experience" (PR, 4–5).

It is indeed ambitious to seek "an essence of the universe which forbids relationship beyond itself." But have we not seen, in instance after instance, that whatever is real is related in some definite way to all other things (PR, 6)? If we would begin with the data of mathematics, logic, science, the arts, religion, and civilization in its historic development, as we have explored them, could we not say that each of these is based on a discovery of some regularity or other? Sometimes it was order of a serial kind, sometimes dialectical, sometimes hierarchical, sometimes harmonious. Each mode of order has various meanings. But always there is some order. Hence metaphysics, if based on order as the essence, could generalize. "The true method of discovery is like the flight of an aeroplane. It starts from the ground of particular observation; it makes a flight in the thin air of imaginative generalization; and it again lands for renewed observation rendered acute by rational interpretation" (*PR,* 7). We have followed this method by observing order in many particular areas, and now we are prepared to try the most general overview. Whitehead claims that metaphysics must have an empirical basis, and that we cannot begin such a study a priori and deduce consequences.

We may be reluctant to take this imaginative flight because in every particular instance of the discovery of order there was also some disorder. Education begins with romance and there is then the contrary of precision. In physical science there is continuity, but then the discontinuity of the quantum theory of energy. In the arts and religion are novel insights that disrupt inherited customs. It is therefore easy to see that our world, particularly when there is strife in society, and lack of relation or antagonism between science and religion, between the arts and morality, might be pictured as chaotic. We sometimes refer to it as higgledy-piggledy, topsy-turvy, and events seem helter-skelter and pell-mell. Many of these jingling expressions come from the late 1500s, before the neat, tidy world of seventeenth-century science and its confidence in stating all order as scientific law. Whitehead takes the earlier world-view as seriously as the later.

The philosophy of organism need not be rejected because of failure to recognize disorder. The subject of cosmology is "order in the universe. . . . For the organic doctrine the problem of order assumes primary importance. . . . Now the correlative of 'order' is 'disorder.' There can be no peculiar meaning in the notion of 'order' unless this contrast holds." Both are given: "'order' means more than givenness . . .; 'disorder' is also 'given.'" There is also no perfect order: "Each actual entity . . . attains its measure of 'order'" (*PR,* 127). We must, as we have in each area, allow for order-disorder.

If this is a philosophy in which order-disorder is the essence of reality, then to be is not only to be in definite relationships but in indefinite relationships also. Just as we found various meanings of hierarchy, dialectic, balance, and particularly of harmony, so we find in the most general and systematic statement of the philosophy of organism, no one meaning of "order."

The total achievement of this philosophy can be interpreted, as we have seen, as the search in each area for the specific order. In each instance, as civilization, there is some harmony, but much disharmony. There are in every instance of order, some given elements blocking the "attainment of the full ideal" (*PR*, 128).

We may have had the misfortune to encounter "order" in the way used ideologically by Communists and Fascists to justify tyranny and to suppress variety and change. The classic model of such oppressive rigidity of class structure is Plato's *Republic*. Whitehead is rejecting this meaning.

The notion of one ideal [order] arises from the disastrous over-moralization of thought under the influence of fanaticism, or pedantry. The notion of a dominant ideal peculiar to each actual entity is Platonic. (*PR*, 128)

A very familiar traditional concept of order is in metaphysical systems that overemphasized the purposiveness observed by Aristotle in organisms. Probably Whitehead means when Aristotle was combined with the biblical concept of one absolute divine power, whose purpose all creatures must serve. That all order is the Creator's order is also rejected. This

philosophy led to a wild overstressing of the notion of final causes during the Christian middle ages; and thence, by a reaction, to the correlative overstressing of the notion of "efficient causes" during the modern scientific period. One task of a sound metaphysics is to exhibit final and efficient causes in their proper relation to each other. (*PR*, 128–29)

We are all familiar with explanations that are systematic in assuming one ground of order. In Marxist systems all behavior has to be interpreted according to economic interests of some social class. In Freudian systems all behavior has to be interpreted according to sex. It might be feared of a philosophy seeking "an essence of the universe" that it might fall into fallacies that attend one-idea'd schemes. The philosophy of organism is not formulated by a fanatic with one *idée fixe*, but secures its unity by observation of variety. It is characteristic of Whitehead to write "Four grounds of 'order' at once emerge" (*PR*, 127). The search for "an essence" does not then imply anything like the "block universe" that so revolted William James.

There are a plurality of "sheer actualities," and all actualities are equally real: "it does not lead us to any higher grade of reality. The coherence which the system seeks to preserve is the discovery that the process, or concrescence, of any one actual entity involves the other actual entities among its components. In this way the obvious solidarity of the world receives its explanation" (*PR*, 10).

Categories

To be presented with a categoreal scheme is to be offered those few most general features of everything there is and of everything that can be reasoned or said. We have already seen Whitehead's philosophy developing out of a struggle between the categories of materialism and of idealism. One scheme has matter, space, motion, etc.; the other has mind, ideas, etc. Because Whitehead's own philosophy had the categoreal conception of forms of definiteness, the Pythagorean heritage, and the conception of organism that is self-creating, the Hegelian heritage, it was necessary to work out his own scheme of categories. It was not arrogance for him to feel deep dissatisfaction with any ready-made scheme. We may find it necessary to compare the categoreal scheme with other more familiar schemes based on substance, and which became, because of Aristotle, the supercategory of many subsequent systems. We have prepared ourselves for the centrality of order-disorder to develop in the scheme what seems most novel and provocative.

To be presented with any categoreal scheme is rather overwhelming because of the extreme condensation of the universal structure of things into ten such as "substance, quantity, quality, relation, place, time, position, state, action and affection." The latter nine are "predicates" of substance, as when we say how much, of what sort, etc., of something. Whitehead, having rejected the subject-predicate logic, required another scheme. Categories apply to everything and are more general than classes. The similarity of Whitehead's to Aristotle's is the effort to achieve completeness. And this is the other reason why reading the dozen pages of *Process and Reality* on the categories is likely to leave even experienced philosophers in a state of bewilderment and stupor. For he presents in quick succession the Category of the Ultimate, eight Categories of Existence, twenty-seven Categories of Explanation, and nine Categoreal Obligations. When there are forty-five categories in all, they are, as Whitehead observed, unintelligible without the illustrations in the rest of *Process and Reality*. Moreover, the connections are difficult to make; and it may even seem that having set forth a scheme, he then ignored it.

Yet Whitehead is clear and lucid about categories. Just before he lists his Categories, in the four types, he gives the clue that he is following the

"Platonic philosophy [in] seek[ing] the forms in facts" (PR, 30). Whitehead had introduced form, in the classical Greek meaning of *eidos*, the complementary of "abstract matter, the *hyle*." What is meant by "form"? Form is "the eternal relatedness" (*SMW*, 238). "To understand *A* is to understand the *how* of a general *scheme of relationship*" (*SMW*, 238–39, italics added).

It is not unfamiliar in the history of philosophy to stress relations as the key to the categories, as did Kant, and it was appropriate since Whitehead defended a relational theory of space and time. What we introduced earlier as "eternal objects" are found in "hierarchic patterns, included and excluded in every variety of discrimination. Another view of the same truth is that every actual occasion is a limitation imposed on possibility . . ." (*SMW*, 251). Whitehead does not pause to illustrate, perhaps because as a geometer it is all too obvious that actual things in space have shapes, such as sphere, pyramid, cube, etc., by which abstract names we discriminate types of solids in an orderly way. Having one surface, or four, or six, are classes of solids; but one level of abstraction, we learn from Whitehead, leads us to another, say enclosure, which is common to the like of these three. But enclosure is of space, which is often taken to be categoreal. We may even choose to regard spatial relations as but one of several, with temporal relations also included in extension. Certainly the most important prelude to Whitehead's work on categories is his theory of space-time. In a relational world there are "categorical determinations" (*SMW*, 252). Whitehead used "categorical" perhaps to suggest necessities, whereas later "categoreal" means only generality.[1] But we need to reflect upon the system as "necessary" (*PR*, 4).

The problem of a categoreal scheme is all the more acute when a philosophy of organism appeals to the participation of the temporal in "the things which are eternal." This is not only a Platonic but a Christian dualism. How can this be explained? The philosophy of organism had made every effort to overcome the modern dualism of mind and matter. Has it fallen back into the ancient dualism?

Why are there not then only two types? Why are there four types of categories? This is a question of the reader of *Process and Reality*, and answered. The best answer is this passage:

Every entity should be a specific instance of one category of existence, every explanation should be a specific instance of categories of explanation, and every obligation should be a specific instance of categoreal obligations. The category of the Ultimate expresses the general principle presupposed in the three more special categories. (*PR*, 31)

If the ultimate is "'creativity,' 'many,' 'one,'" then what is ultimately beneath and behind is ordering, by which there is process from disjunction to conjunction. That is, how can "the many enter into complex unity" (*PR*, 31)? If there is ordering there must be a relating, and therefore things related, the relata, brought together. There is a necessity implicit here, which we need further to develop.

There must be something to be related. We sometimes call it "ontology" when we discuss what there is. We have already considered the eternal objects and actualities, but keep open the question of whether there are only these two kinds of things. There must be the ways things are related, and ask the question of how? We have already considered the mechanistic explanation of forces attracting and repelling one another, an explanation to which Whitehead provided an alternative organic cosmology. But it is not complete to say what there is or how related. There must be, in addition to *what* and *how*, a *why* of the process, and some indication of purpose among the categories of obligation.

There are then in Whitehead's Categoreal Scheme justifications of *four sets of categories.* Central to all of them is order-disorder, which we might write "disorder-order" since creativity is ultimate, but as a formative element together with many and one. What is the nature of things such that there can be the kinds of order we experience? Not even God is a category: "the Divine Ordering" is a "derivative notion" of the scheme, along with social and personal orders, and the seriality of time (*PR*, 4 and 46–53; we have taken "derivative notions" to express presuppositions of the system). The scheme is tested in experience for adequacy. "It means that the texture of observed experience . . . is such that all related experience must exhibit the same texture. Thus the philosophic scheme should be 'necessary' in the sense of bearing in itself its own warrant of universality throughout all experience . . ." (*PR*, 5).

In these many ways the categoreal scheme is a conception fitted to absorb and subsume dualities as polar tensions.

The Category of the Ultimate: Creativity, Many, One

"A metaphysics is a description. . . . The tests of accuracy are logical coherence, adequacy, and exemplification" (*RM*, 88–89). When from the perspective of religion Whitehead outlined a categoreal scheme, it is not only forms but "creativity" that is important. *Science and the Modern World* had stressed the determination of form. *Religion in the Making* includes the forms but begins with the indetermination of creativity. "There are many ways of analyzing the universe, conceived as that which is comprehensive of all there is. In a description it is thus necessary to correlate these different routes of analysis" (*RM*, 89).

"Such formative elements are not themselves actual and passing; they are the factors which are either non-actual or non-temporal, disclosed in the analysis of what is both actual and temporal" (*RM*, 89). This helps distinguish a categoreal form from less general sorts when we consider three "formative elements:"

1. The creativity whereby the actual world has its character of temporal passage to novelty.
2. The realm of ideal entities, or forms, which are in themselves not actual, but are such that they are exemplified in everything that is actual, according to some proportion of relevance.
3. The actual but non-temporal entity whereby the indetermination of mere creativity is transmuted into a determinate freedom. This non-temporal actual entity is what men call God—the supreme God of rationalized religion. (*RM*, 90)

"Creativity" is introduced in *Religion in the Making* as one of "three formative elements," along with eternal objects and God. The three together account for the order of the actual entities. The passage is, as many of the most important in Whitehead, telegraphic: the first is explained as the "indetermination of mere creativity." By "indeterminate" is apparently meant something that has no characteristic that is constant. Because constantly changing, it is called "protean," and since it is no more "actual" than the forms, it may be the indefinite contrasted to forms of definiteness, and in that respect something like the traditional concept of "prime matter." Since it is only one of three formative elements, we can also say that it is not "God" as usually conceived in the West, for it is what is denied, a ground of God. Although the question "Who made God?" appears a joke, theologians now seriously consider a "God beyond God." We cannot speak of creativity as many, or one, and we cannot ascribe qualities to it, for they are all forms of definiteness, and although creativity is associated with "temporal passage into novelty," it cannot be past, present, and future or temporally related as an event to other events. It is very difficult then to say anything, when quantity, quality, and relation do not apply. Perhaps therefore it would have been better to say "the primordial" rather than "the ultimate."

Creativity is "protean" and cannot be an actual entity, but it can be grasped in the temporal world in which there are "a multiplicity of occasions of actualization" (*RM*, 92, 91). Whitehead might have paused, as he sometimes does, to remind us of the god Proteus, who takes on all forms. "Protean" means exceedingly variable, even capable of all determination.

"Creativity" may suggest "Creator." Whitehead is aware of the suggestion and warns against it, because it is not what is intended. The Creator is "external . . . eliciting this final togetherness out of nothingness." Creativity "is a metaphysical principle belonging to the nature of things, that there is nothing in the universe other than instances of this passage and components of these instances." Whereas the Creator is commonly thought to be external, we are here considering a theory of "Immanent Creativity." The Creator is "transcendent," but immanent creativity implies that each event is self-creative. The Creator secures a new creation, and in this one aspect, so also does creativity: "it does convey the origination of novelty" (*AI*, 303). Whitehead could have appealed to the strain of biblical thought that leads to the doctrine of the "hidden" God beyond the God that is "revealed," and sometimes leads mystical theologians to identify the primordial divine with chaos, but the text dwells upon disagreement with the orthodox tradition, and it must be added, Whitehead responded favorably to mystical heretics.

In traditional Western philosophies the ultimate is perfect and eternal. Categoreal schemes were suited if not devised to show all finite substances derivative from an infinite substance. God, for example, is not only "the supreme being," He is said to be "Being Itself." Whitehead's ultimate is said not to be the Creator but creativity. This will not seem unfamiliar, he suggests, to those who know Eastern rather than Western thought. Ultimately, according to the *Tao Te Ching,* to which Whitehead may be referring, the *Tao,* translated "Way," cannot be named.[2] We read also in the *Upanishads* of the ultimate Brahma, which can be characterized only negatively.[3] Had Whitehead written in our generation, when some of us, particularly the young, are more familiar with Eastern than with Western metaphysics, more specific references could be helpful. But the idea is not difficult. We must begin with something indefinite, which is to be defined. For what becomes actual presupposes something which can be actualized, that is, something potential. If one has this notion, there is no need or possibility even of saying much about it. It is present in Western philosophy, but not enough is made of it, or it is concealed rather than given the primordial place. "In all philosophic theory there is an ultimate which is actual in virtue of its accidents. It is only then capable of characterization through its accidental embodiments and apart from these is devoid of actuality" (*PR*, 10–11). As creativity is "nonactual" we are reminded that earlier we read of eternal objects and possibles. Religious thinkers conceived ideas as aspects of the vision of God; they were "real, yet waiting to be realized" (*SMW*, 275). It is very difficult to talk of "reality behind the scene" and "ground of rationalty" (*SMW*, 256–57) because we are talking the language of the "scene" in rational patterns, hence the metaphysician must talk metaphorically, saying what creativity is like in some ways, yet not in others.

Particularly in reading Whitehead's metaphysical system on creativity, it is necessary to keep in mind what became increasingly evident. This is both our lack of insight and the weakness of language. Although nothing appears to be more technical and therefore well defined and reasoned, creativity must be the least defined, and as the ultimate ground of reason, can be the ultimate irrationality. It is as true of the ultimate as what is said of God: "No reason can be given for [its] nature . . ., because that . . . is the ground of rationality" (*SMW*, 257). The "nature" accompanying creativity is the many and the one.

Whitehead reminds us of our experiences with language. We never quite say what we mean or mean what we say. The truest thing we can ever say is "I can't say it" or "it is unsayable." Says Whitehead: "Language is thoroughly indeterminate, by reason of the fact that every occurrence presupposes some systematic type of environment" (*PR*, 18). So the paradox deepens: the categories are to state the systematic context within which we can be clear and coherent. Yet the categoreal scheme begins with creativity, which is a metaphorical expression, and only in hints and suggestions can we guess what it may be. Whitehead could have used a scriptural text, for his writing shows deep absorption of the King James Version: "we see through a glass darkly."

Creare, the Latin verb, means "to bring forth, beget, produce" (*PR*, 324). To produce, as a female and male together make an offspring, may be the metaphor behind the coupling of many to produce one. The metaphor was adopted from Plato, whence Whitehead draws reference to the "foster mother of all becoming" (*AI*, 192). Is it legitimate to apply terms from biological process to the ultimate, and to give the connotation to the "it" of creativity that we can think of it as the sexual opposites, "she" and "he"? The justification is that there is "no meaning of creativity apart from its creatures" (*PR*, 344).

Whitehead had a high regard for "the creative person," and we have seen that his whole philosophy may be read as a theory of how to produce "creative" people. He had high regard for artistic creativity, and he allowed the category "creativity" to suggest "creative" artistry. Whitehead began his discussion of "causal efficacy" with the potter shaping the clay, and gives us a suggestion why he thought of biological productivity. We are all begotten and born, but only a few become creative artists. Hence the category should be drawn from what is most general, subhuman as well as human. Generation, in organic terms, can be more easily generalized.

Yet when generalized, there is a falsehood if we are literal. Generation is temporal, and creativity is "nontemporal," yet as basis of actuality, linked with time. The paradox is resolved by saying that creativity is "disclosed in the analysis of what is both actual and temporal . . ." (*RM,* 89). This could have been clarified, if following Taoism Whitehead had spoken of the indefinite and nameless creativity and the definite and named creativity.

It is again paradoxical to call Creativity "the universal of universals characterizing ultimate matter of fact" (*PR,* 31). We know what Whitehead means by "universal," namely, a "form of definiteness." How can the indefinite be definite? We are not to think of this contradiction, unless we consider a form as possible. Then "the universal of universals" should be read "the possibility of possibles." Then to seek the "forms in the facts" would mean to see the underlying possibility out of which issues actuality. But then why do we need creativity as well as a realm of possibilities? Since the two are coupled to account for process, the reason is that there must be a concrete "ultimate behind all forms," and the concrete is the basis of the abstract (*PR,* 30).

Another paradox shows how misleading it is to try to state the categoreal scheme as a continuation of Western metaphysics. This is that this "ultimate" is said to be comparable *both* to "pure matter" and to "pure actuality." In our systematic tradition of medieval Scholasticism this is absurd and even blasphemous. Here Whitehead is most helpful:

Pure matter, without form, is said by Aristotle to be "passive receptivity." This Whitehead does not intend. The point in common between pure matter and creativity is being "without a character of its own." At the "base of actuality" is flux, in Heraclitus' term "never the same twice, though always with the stable element of divine ordering." This is Heraclitus' logos.

Whereas in traditional Western metaphysics there can be no matter without form, and the form is individuated by matter, in Whitehead's scheme the form is only possible. The form must come from something. Could the something prior be creativity? It is an exciting alternative that form comes from matter, a novel position recently uncovered in that genius of the Renaissance, Guillaume Postel.[4] Yet if we take seriously the quotation from Milton that we begin with chaos, which then, as a trackless waste, begins to show definiteness, we could go so far with Whitehead. Then "forms *of* definiteness" may be "forms *from* indefiniteness." This Whitehead does not say explicitly, but since the creative is not only active but "spontaneous" and "novel," if creativity itself is "an element of confusion" (*AI,* 369), then what would contrast to confusion is some measure of clarity and distinctness. Then creativity could be the matrix of the creatures. But how far is this maternity to be extended? We can easily accept creativity as mother of nature, but is it (or rather she) also mother of God? We shall see in the next chapter Whitehead's encouragement of imaginative metaphors in religion, but here we must halt with nature. "Nature is never complete. It is always passing beyond itself. This is the creative advance of nature" (*PR,* 443).

"Creativity" is spoken of in both positive and negative terms. The positive characterizations are "spontaneous," "free," "novel," and above all "productive." The negatives are "formless," "indefinite," "indetermi-nate," "incomplete." Because we read one characterization as grammatically and logically negative is no reason why we should not convert the meaning into something positive. For example, when we read "its character lacks determinateness" we may think "sheer raw energy" (*RM,* 92). Creativity is, after all, a "formative element" and not merely an ultimate unknowable.

There is a great benefit in having creativity as the ultimate. If we regard God as the ultimate, then God is responsible for evil as well as good. But if we posit only "ultimate activity," then we can keep God as a principle discriminating good from evil. God can be "aim towards 'order'" and there is something to be ordered (*PR,* 373–74). Creativity is prior to order and disorder, and prior to existence itself. This allows us to recognize in creation as many kinds of existence as there are, not merely the "two orders of existence," actual entities and eternal objects, which "stand out with a certain extreme finality" (*PR,* 33). With an underlying feeling of unity and plurality in activity we can recognize polarities without falling into irreconcilable dualism. We proceed to the great problem of the "form of creation" (*MT,* 114). Creativity has given the ground of creation. "The process of creation is the form of unity of the Universe" (*AI,* 231).

The Categories of *What, How, Why:*
Categories of Existence, Explanation, and Obligations

We come now to the "qualifications of creativity" or the "creatures of creativity." The important central focus is that there are things related in such ways that we can know orders, that there are active relatings, and that there is direction toward satisfaction. The category, or perhaps "super-category," which collectively links the ultimate, "'creativity,' 'one,' 'many,'" to existence, explanation, and obligation, is ordering. To state categories is to say how we find the world to be ordered or what we think is the structure of the universe. For there to be a system or a categoreal scheme is the assertion of an overall order, whatever the other categories are, including various orders. The philosophy of organism affirms an ordered creation. It is a world that shows mutual relations between real things and one that cannot be "shivered into a multitude of disconnected substantial things . . ." (*AI*, 170).

The categories other than the ultimate are those that might be called *what, how,* and *why.* This use of adverbs is found largely explicitly in the brief pages on the categories. But such a simplification enables us to concentrate on ordering, which must be relating "whats" in definite ways, which are "hows" and to accomplish certain aims, which are "whys."

In one of the earliest metaphysical discussions, the question is of the "*what* of matter of fact" and the "particular *how*" and when God is introduced as dividing the Good from the Evil, the *why* (*SMW*, 256–58). The metaphysical *what, how,* and *why* are not merely some one thing, some one way, some one reason, but it is explicitly inescapable and "necessary" that there be some of a range of *whats, hows,* and *whys.*

Discussing categories Whitehead mentions *which* or *what* or *how.* These relatives are needed to discuss an entity (*PR*, 31). The *which* refers to "specific determinations," a reference to eternal objects, the "*what*" to "actual entities" (also called "actual occasions") or "final realities" and other types of existence (*PR*, 32–33). The "*how*" is used in the categories of explanation. Among twenty-seven is the ninth: "That *how* an actual entity *becomes* constitutes *what* that actual entity *is;* so that the two descriptions of an actual entity are not independent. Its 'being' is consti-tuted by its 'becoming.' This is the 'principle of process'" (*PR*, 34–35). To account for becoming as "a creative advance into novelty" we must also have aim or purpose (*PR*, 42). The relative "*why*" is therefore appropriate. Several of these are included among the nine categoreal obligations. All of them concern "integration," "satisfaction," "coalescence," determination, but particularly the achievement of harmony as an aim, and freedom to determine oneself in anticipation of the *"relevant* future" (*PR,* 39–41).

Order is even more explicit in "some derivative notions," for here we have the "divine ordering," or "'God' . . . the timeless source of all order . . ." (*PR,* 46–47). *Process and Reality* is unlike theories of the Creator, to Whom is ascribed the radical origination of essence and existence (*PR,* 343–44). That is, the philosophy of organism does not agree that God creates the *"what"* and imposes the *"how"* of law upon chaos and is thus the only responsible *"why"* of creation. Yet this philosophy also affirms divine ordering as not only the "refreshment and companionship at which religions aim," but the purposiveness of final causes, and in this limited sense "the creator of each temporal actual entity" (*PR,* 343).

Just as Aristotle, taking his predecessors into account, came upon a doctrine of four causes, so Whitehead has four classes or groups of categories. One way to think of Aristotle and Whitehead together is to regard both as seekers after philosophic adequacy in a first philosophy that is also theology. Aristotle insisted upon material, formal, efficient, and final causes, and one way Aristotelians have of studying anything is to seek that out of which, that sort or type in which, that efficient agency by which, and that for which a thing is. Whitehead also studies his predecessors to produce an outline of cosmic adequacy. Although he is busy telling us how Aristotle both created and perverted the tradition, he does not point out that his four kinds of categories have a resemblance to Aristotle's four causes. Is not creativity likened to prime matter, the out of which? Are not eternal objects very close to Aristotle's forms? Are not explanations frequently appeals to efficient causes? And the likeness between Aristotle's prime mover and Whitehead's God is in providing the lure and drawing power toward ideal ends.

If the four causes apply to all actualities, and are aspects abstractable from every process, then the objection vanishes that Aristotle tried to classify where we should not classify. It is also of great value to see Whitehead's final response to the hierarchical order developed from Aristotle by the medieval schemes of order.

Whitehead distinguishes sharply between "category" and "class," as does *Modern English Usage.* H. W. Fowler writes that "category should be used by no one who is not prepared to state (1) that he does not mean *class,* and (2) that he knows the difference between the two. . . ."[5] "Category" is not a "stylish" substitute for the "working word" class. Whitehead is prepared to state the difference. The generalizations of philosophy "almost fail to classify by reason of their universal application. For example, all things are involved in the creative advance of the Universe, that is, in the general temporality which affects all things, even if at all times they remain self-identical" (*AI,* 183). Whitehead contrasts his category of time, which does not lead to classification in the same direct way in which "consideration of weight led Aristotle to his four-fold classification." Weight gave Aristotle his cosmology of things of heaven, things which tend upward, things which tend downward, and earth (*AI,* 181). Whitehead's categories do not cut up the world into levels, and this gives us an answer as to why he explicitly denies levels of being.

There is no going behind actual entities [the final real things of which the world is made] to find anything more real. They differ among themselves. God is an actual entity, and so is the most trivial puff of existence in far-off empty space. But, though there are *gradations of importance, and diversities of function,* yet in the principles which actuality exemplifies *all are on the same level. The final facts are, all alike, actual entities;* and these actual entities are drops of experience, complex and interdependent. (*PR,* 27–28, italics added)

Along with the denial of one dominant ordering of all events to one final purpose comes this explicit departure from the Aristotelian and Neo-Platonic scheme of making each lower level material for the next highest level. The higher is not, according to Whitehead, more real than the lower. In the philosophy of organism, plants may have the function of being food for animals, and animals may be food for men, yet metaphysically plants and animals can be for their own sake.

Although we may find it necessary to compare and contrast categoreal schemes, and Whitehead does make such contrasts to help us understand his scheme, the evidence for it must be, as he says, direct experience or intuition. We might well ask a metaphysician who offers us a new set of categories, what is the source of your confidence? The basic assurance in Whitehead's case was not primarily that he had studied other philosophers, but that he used their questions and answers in consulting his own experience. Because of the equivalence of nature and experience, the modes of existence are modes of experience. One very revealing passage shows us how a metaphysician finds his "modes of experience" in listening to music.

. . . In some concert hall there is the immediate volume of sound in the immediate specious present. There is the symphonic form which is dominating the successive moments of experience. There is the sense of creative genius from which this realized example of symphonic form is derived. There is the sense of multiplicity of creative genius—the artists in the orchestra, the conductor, the composer. There is the sense of the variety of static forms immediately realized: the forms of instruments, the spatial distribution of the orchestra, the mathematical analysis of each momentary sound, the musical score. In the end we are left with four main modes of characterizing experience. There are, in the first place, three main aspects within aesthetic experience: the sense of genius, the sense of disclosure, the sense of frustration. We also retain three aspects of matter of fact; namely, the experiences of unity, of multitude, of transition. (*MT,* 115–16)

What are the "four main modes of characterizing experience"? And what are the "three aspects of matter of fact"? And what are "three primary grounds of division"? These are ways to put the metaphysical question so that we too can consult experience. We may not be able to find exact parallelisms between them, but one mode of experiencing, say the first, may be the ultimate that cannot be one of the three "aspects of matter of fact" and one of the three "primary grounds of division." Certainly the categoreal scheme concerns "unity, multiplicity, [and] transition." And categories do concern "Clarity and Vagueness, Order and Disorder, The Good and the Bad." Certainly the difficulty of categories is that they are found together and therefore difficult to distinguish.

The Categoreal Scheme of *Process and Reality* is Whitehead's specialist effort to state the system in contrast to other great systems known to specialists. It is the subject of a dozen expositions and criticisms, and is one of the most perplexing mazes for young technicians to thread on their way to the doctorate. Some aspect of the scheme is frequently the subject of a dissertation.

Whitehead provided other versions of the system in applications that can be appreciated more readily by any person of civilized concern in *Adventures of Ideas,* Parts 2 and 3, especially in Chapter 9, "Science and Philosophy," Chapter 11, "Objects and Subjects," and in *Modes of Thought,* Parts 1 and 2, especially in Chapter 3, "Understanding," and Chapter 4, "Perspective," Chapter 5, "Forms of Process," and Chapter 6, "Civilized Universe." These are far better pieces of writing than *Process and Reality.* But it is the masterpiece, however flawed, and we must interpret its categoreal scheme. What has not been observed earlier is that a use of the other works makes *Process and Reality* palatable.

The *Whats*: Categories of Existence

"What is there?" is a fundamental metaphysical question, and one way of answering is to give a set of categories as names. This Whitehead does in Categories of Existence. By contrast, the later two sets of categories are not names but propositions.

The general term "existence" is used of eight "types," but the first, "Actual Entities" or "Actual Occasions," are called "Final *Realities.*" We might then ponder whether we could not as well call these the "categories of reality." This would be better, because then we are saying that eternal objects are real potentials for actualization. They are real though not actual and do not exist in space-time. For reality is not limited to entities in space-time. The clear intention is not merely to detail an inventory of eight sorts of things that may be called "real," but to show how these sorts are related to each other. ". . . Actual entities and eternal objects stand out with a certain extreme finality. The other types of existence have a certain intermediate character" (*PR,* 33). Let us therefore examine the relationships among the various types, much as we did when first considering eternal objects and actuality, when earlier we had to introduce prehensions between actualities. Thereby we can test the promise of the philosophy of organism to represent to us a real cosmic order.

The things of everyday reality, which we consider in the philosophy of organism, can be divided and are therefore made up of parts. If there are many things on the macrocosmic level, there must be even more on the microcosmic level. The question "what is real?" includes the question "of what are things made?" "The final facts, . . . actual entities . . . are drops of experience, complex and interdependent" (*PR,* 28). This is a metaphysical claim made with no more appeal than we have already seen to past philosophy and to science: "Mathematical physics also accepts the atomistic doctrine of Democritus" (*PR,* 471). When "many" was introduced as an aspect of the ultimate, this marked a chosen beginning point that is axiomatically true. At least we can safely begin here without demanding proof.

The ultimate creature is a monad, a simple unit that *becomes.* "Each monadic creature is a mode of the process of 'feeling' the world, of housing the world in one unit of complex feeling, in every way determinate. Such a unit is an 'actual occasion'; it is the ultimate creature derivative from the creative process" (*PR,* 124). It is a quantum "constituted by its totality of relationships and cannot move. Also the creature cannot have any external adventures, but only the internal adventure of becoming. Its birth is its end" (*PR*, 124).

An "actual entity" is a rather indefinite sort of thing, and we need only assume here how it happens independent of spatial relations to other entities, though it is only the temporal relations stressed explicitly as "a conditioned actual entity of the temporal world," and as such excluding God (*PR*, 135). It is referred to both as "particular" and as "individual" (*PR*, 76, 135). Each is an "individual for its own sake; and thereby transcends the rest of actuality" (*PR*, 135).

Are entities to be considered material or mental? Although they are called "monads" they are not, as Leibniz's, mental, and although compared with Democritus' atoms and physical quanta, they are not material. They are neither mental nor material yet capable of being both. This certainly is superior to idealistic and materialistic philosophies that create the problem of relationship between two utterly different sorts of substance. The term to refer to such a position, in contrast to mind-body dualism, is "neutral monism."

"According to the ontological principle there is nothing which floats into the world from nowhere. Everything in the actual world is referable to some actual entity" (*PR*, 373). This is a more general principle than that asserted in materialistic systems: out of nothing, nothing comes (Lucretius, disciple of Democritus, said, "Ex nihilo, nihil fit").[6] Whitehead summarizes his axiom as "no actual entity, then no reason" (*PR*, 28). The basis of "philosophic thought" must then be "the most concrete elements in our experience." ". . . Apart from things that are actual, there is nothing—nothing either in fact or in efficacy. Everything is positively somewhere in actuality, and in potency everywhere" (*PR*, 64). We shall need this in the next section because the *whats* of actuality have in them the basis for the *hows* (*PR*, 36–37). Yet there cannot be *whats* apart from *hows*, for being is becoming.

An actuality, this dog, is actual in doing something. The class *canis* does nothing, and in this sense the class is not actual. "The appeal to a class to perform the services of a proper entity is exactly analogous to an appeal to an imaginary terrier to kill a real rat" (*PR*, 348). This may tell us dramatically that only an actuality can act, and that "reality" is characterized as "power" (*PR*, 89–91). Yet are eternal objects powers if they do nothing? Whitehead must have in reserve a distinction between actual-real and potential-real.

There are "Prehensions, *or* Concrete Facts of Relatedness" (*PR*, 32). "The first analysis of an actual entity, into its most concrete elements, discloses it to be a concresence of prehensions, which have originated in its process of becoming" (*PR*, 35, the tenth principle of explanation, which might better be placed as an account of the second category of existence).

Above we noted that actualities allow us to analyze them into parts, but whatever parts there are can be combined into wholes. Opposite to axiomatic disjunction is conjunction. In the former case we are reminded of atoms and quanta. In the latter, once we recognize prehensions, we are reminded of cells. "The philosophy of organism is a cell-theory of actuality. Each ultimate unit of fact is a cell-complex, not analyzable into components with equivalent completeness of actuality" (*PR*, 334). We need both the atomic truth that a whole can be analyzed into parts, and the cellular truth that a whole is more than its parts and not simply, or without remainder, reducible to them. Whitehead's way of saying this is to include real concrete relations between "the various elements of the universe out of which it arises" (*PR*, 335). Prehension is genetically a "process of appropriation of a particular element. . . ."

The ultimate elements of the universe, thus appropriated, are the already-constituted actual entities, and the eternal objects. All the actual entities are positively prehended, but only a selection of the eternal objects. (*PR*, 335)

Prehensions are prehensions of other actual entities or prehensions of eternal objects. The former are called "physical prehensions," the latter "conceptual prehensions."

Prehensions lead categorically from simple or pure prehensions to complex or impure prehensions. There can be, for example, hybrid prehensions, which are examples of "prehension by one subject of a conceptual prehension, or of an 'impure' prehension, belonging to the mentality of another subject" (*PR*, 163). This leads to "new entities" of such types "as novel propositions and generic contrasts . . ." (*PR*, 335). It is puzzling why a philosopher should make the claim that each actuality can appropriate whatever actual there might be of whatever type. Apparently this would not lead, as appropriation of all possibles, to contradictories. Actuality or existence is not, as with some existentialists, absurd. The problem is how there can be a universe. We might be tempted by other philosophies that have fewer types of existence and nothing like prehensions. How can one thing include another, or prehend it into its constitution? "This is the problem of the solidarity of the universe" (*PR*, 88).

Actual entities involve each other by reason of their prehensions of each other. There are thus real individual facts of the togetherness of actual entities, which are real, individual, and particular, in the same sense in which actual entities and the prehensions are real, individual and particular. Any such particular fact of togetherness among actual entities is called a "nexus." (*PR,* 29–30)

What is a nexus? Or, to use the plural, What are nexūs? This should be far easier to say than to give an account of a formative element because we are said to have here one of "the most concrete elements in our experience" (*PR,* 27). Whitehead should tell us that "nexus" is derived from the Latin verb meaning to bind, and it was in the sense of "binding one thing out of two, bringing together two things into one" (Seneca, *Letter* 67). Examples abound in Latin literature, as branches of a tree, the arms of wrestlers, the ropes tied together to form a net, and the idea is extended by Tacitus to the "network of law." (3 Ann. 28.6). The only concrete illustration of a nexus offered by Whitehead himself is of a chair, and the irony is that, although we commonly think of it as simple, it is complex because it has parts, and was experienced in the past, yet we refer to it as present. What is the "real chair"? Only by taking the historic routes of its manufacture, transportation, uses can we have more than an aspect (*PR,* 97–99). The "route" means that the chair is an "event," in that it has "successive occasions of its life-history" (*PR,* 124).

A nexus is complex: if a chair illustrates it, then obviously, however complex, it is relatively simple. Compared to what? We must use our imagination here. A chair may be part of the kitchen furniture as used in a home, together with a table, etc. This idea of levels of complexity is that of "regular trains of waves, individual electrons, protons, individual molecules, societies of molecules such as inorganic bodies, living cells, and societies of cells such as vegetable and animal bodies" (*PR,* 150). A more complex level than the nexus is the society.

Some nexūs (Latin plural, whose English might be "nexuses") are societies, and it is here that we recognize explicitly that the philosophy of organism is an account of order. There are "social orders" and some social orders are personal orders. "A 'society,' in the sense in which that term is here used, is a nexus with social order; and an 'enduring object,' or 'enduring creature' is a society whose social order has taken on the special form of 'personal order'" (*PR,* 50).

A nexus is called a society because of its form: (1) there is "definiteness of each of its included actual entities," (2) this common form "arises in each member of the nexus" because of prehending other members of the nexus, and (3) these "prehensions impose that condition of reproduction" because they include "positive feelings of that common form" (*PR*, 50–51).

Does it help much to be told that this concept is like Aristotle's "substantial form" and is "a complex eternal object" (*PR*, 51)? And does it really help to be told that "a non-social nexus is what answers to the notion of 'chaos'" (*PR*, 112)? What he suggests but does not make fully explicit, is that what he means by "society" is something like a biological organism. If it is the case that each cell shares characteristics of being human, and of being male or female, then the definition would find an appropriate example.

The crucial distinction is made here by *Process and Reality* between "merely mathematical conception of order" and a society, illustrated by an organism, which is "self-sustaining." Only the latter "has its own reason" (*PR*, 137).

Whitehead does illustrate "personal order," but first we must inquire into why only some social orders are personal orders.

Although a social order is not a "merely mathematical" order, the language and techniques of relational logic are used in defining the seriality of the genetic relations between the members of a personal order.

When A and B are two members of a nexus, and B inherits from A and from all on that side of a "cut," then we have the defining characteristic of a linear order. It is this nexus that is an "enduring object" (*PR*, 51).

Is it now obvious that defining "order" as a relation that is asymmetrical and transitive was an analytic tool needed in synthetic metaphysics? If not explicit, is it also evident that there is a "connexity" of the nexus? That is, given A and B, any two members of such a serial nexus, must it be either B inheriting from A, or A inheriting from B?

But why call such an order "personal"? Whitehead recognizes that "unfortunately 'person' suggests the notion of consciousness"; all that is meant is "person" in "the legal sense of that term." A *persona* in Latin may mean simply that a nexus "sustains a character." Since an ordinary physical object does that, Whitehead means that in addition to the characteristic of ordinary physical objects, he means being "analyzable into strands of enduring objects." These are also called "corpuscular societies," which stresses again the organic nature of this system (*PR*, 52). But how do we as human persons fit into the system?

. . . The life of man is an historic route of actual occasions which in a marked degree . . . inherit from each other. That set of occasions, dating from his first acquirement of the Greek language and including all those occasions up to his

loss of any adequate knowledge . . . constitutes a society in reference to . . . a
somewhat trivial element of order. . . . (PR, 137)

Perhaps a more important element of order would be the ordering
secured by using one's native language. Would that not be an example of
one crucial and dominating structure "in virtue of which a man is
considered to be the same enduring person from birth to death" (PR,
137)? This raises the very interesting question of whether a "conceptual
scheme" is an ordering essential to being a human person. Perhaps the
categories of a metaphysics, including a logic, and hierarchy of values are
structurally definitive of human personhood.

Of "Multiplicities, or Modes of Pure Disjunctions of Diverse Entities"
we learn much less (PR, 33). Most philosophers who, like Whitehead,
have logical systems, make much of logical classes. A multiplicity is a set,
or entities which have a characteristic in common or which "satisfy at least
one condition which no other entity satisfies" (PR, 36). Because a set does
nothing, is not an *actuality*. A multiplicity, to which a class name applies,
has no continuing ordering as do societies and persons.

No account of what there is can omit propositions. The categoreal
scheme must recognize this "new kind of entity" (PR, 282) and, rather
than assume, as do most logicians, that which in language we call a
"statement," such as a sentence, expresses a proposition that is capable of
being true or false, the metaphysician asks how such a thing can be. A
proposition arises from our prehension of eternal objects and our physical
prehension of actual occasions. We may think when we make a statement
about a particular fact that this concerns only the fact, but "every definite
entity requires a systematic universe to supply its requisite status" (PR,
17). Whitehead supplies no example, but to use an illustration already
familiar, "This is a red ball" presupposes that there is no absurdity in a red
thing being spherical. We have, the argument goes, presupposed the
realm of possibles, the eternal objects, and we make a particular factual
claim that this actuality, or enduring object, illustrates these compatible
characteristics. Obviously the proposition "does not refer to the universe in
all its detail" (PR, 17), but the doctrine is that a proposition is "a hybrid
between pure potentialities and actualities" (PR, 282).

From this theory it follows that a proposition is only a "partial truth"
and not rigidly either "true or false." We are invited to reflect on the
indeterminacy of our language. To continue with our example: What is
"this"? Which exact shade of "red"? Where and when is the "ball," how
large, and who put it where it is? Why should we be interested in it, and is

the ball bouncing, or falling, or stationary? Is this not what we are learning to consider in the "accurate apprehension of the metaphysical background" of the universe which cannot be expressed in ordinary sentences but requires what the categoreal scheme provides, a redesigning of language (*PR*, 16–20)? We have unfortunately become familiar with subject-predicate propositions, and we are inured to them as models of clarity, and without criticism we tend to overlook the inadequate metaphysics. ". . . Consider the type of propositions such as 'The grass is green' and 'The whale is big.' This subject-predicate form of statement seems so simple, leading straight to a metaphysical first principle; and yet in these examples it conceals such complex, diverse meanings" (*PR*, 20).

The theory of propositions gives an "objective" status in a double way because thinking is participating both in a timeless realm of possibilities and in an actual realm of particular events. We can say what a thing happens to be, what it may be, what it must be, what it was, what it will be, and also what it is not. The example Whitehead uses suggests the proposition "Napoleon *won* the Battle of Waterloo," which happens to be false historically but as a proposition this is imaginatively interesting. It suggests "the possibilities of another course of history" (*PR*, 282). Whitehead uses the language of a playwright (his example is from Shakespeare) who uses propositions such as "to be, or not to be . . ." as "a mere lure for feeling" (*PR*, 281). It is therefore intelligible for Whitehead to say that it is more important for a proposition to be interesting than for it to be true (*AI*, 313).

Not only does Whitehead make a great place for the arts, as we saw above, for fiction and drama in the use of language, but here is the ground for his high esteem of the aesthetic approach to reality. As artists say, comparing different colors on a palette, they "feel" different. Whitehead's world may be general when it is expressed as a categoreal scheme, but it is meant to call our attention to vivid particularities.

Even when reading poetry Whitehead was thinking of the categories illustrated in the poet's apprehension of the world. As we saw, the metaphysician was thinking even while listening to music; so in reading Shelley and Wordsworth, his attention was called to "these six [for "five"] notions, change, value, eternal objects, endurance, organism, interfusion" (*SMW*, 127). (A Whiteheadian hermeneutics depends on metaphysical categories.)

It is evident to Whitehead that the poets have a more adequate categoreal scheme than do the physicists. It was not only Democritus who accounted for the universe as atoms and the void; Descartes said matter and motion but added God and minds. Why does Whitehead, by contrast, develop such a complex system? Here is a mathematical physicist who finds the poets more faithful to experience than are the physicists. Therefore he must devise a categoreal scheme adequate to both the poetic and physical points of view, and to the religious point of view.

"Whats" then mean: if X is real, then it is either an actual entity or a prehension or a nexus or a subjective form or an eternal object or a proposition or a multiplicity of disjunction or a contrast. This is an extremely generous recognition of what can legitimately follow the existential claim introduced by "There is." "Actual entities" do indeed occupy the first place, followed by "Prehensions, *or* Concrete Facts of Relatedness." Since an Actual Entity must be related to a past, the full reality must be both of an actual entity and its prehensions. There are both private and public matters of fact. There are both potentials, forms of definiteness, as well as actualities, specific determinations of fact.

In the delightful essay "Activity" in *Modes of Thought* comes Whitehead's final published reflection about what there is. Here is another decisive rejection of forms as "really real." Potentials are only one type of reals. But are there only seven other types? Are there but eight, as we are told in "Categories of Existence" (*PR,* 32–33)? No. "We cannot exhaust such types of existence because there are an unending number of them" (*MT,* 95).

We may not then conclude an exposition of "Categories of Existence" with the notion that there are only eight kinds. Whitehead, at the age of seventy-seven, shows us new approaches to metaphysics. ". . . In order to understand Actuality, we must ask, What is character? and What is it that has character?" This would begin the inquiry with qualities (*MT,* 97). In studying the "fundamental characterizations of our experience" we find "three pairs of opposites—Clarity and Vagueness, Order and Disorder, The Good and the Bad. Our endeavor to understand Creation should start from these modes of experience" (*MT,* 103). Of these pairs, Order and Disorder seem fundamental because the achievement of any excellence requires order (*MT,* 103–8). Yet "life degenerates when enclosed within the shackles of mere conformation. A power of incorporating vague and disorderly elements of experience is essential for the advance into novelty" (*MT,* 109).

The *Hows*: Categories of Explanation

The movement of thought from the ultimate to the categories of existence is the movement from the undifferentiated (creativity, many, one) to the eight *whats*. It is understandable that there should be differentiated kinds of reals, but why so many more kinds of *hows* than of *whats?* The use of "explanation" might suggest that the move from *what* to *how* is a move from the objective, what things are, to the subjective, how we feel and consciously judge; but this can be quickly refuted because "Subjective Forms, *or* Private Matters of Fact" occur among the *whats,* to balance "Nexūs (plural of Nexus), *or* Public Matters of Fact," and although species of subjective forms occur among categories of explanation, most of the *hows* are no less objectively real, being concerned with the cosmic process.

The reason for the astonishing number, several times the usual Aristotelian list of *all* categories, that is ten, more or less, is probably that "explanation" concerns answering the question "How do actualities act in relation to each other?" Probably the Aristotelian model led Whitehead to state the *whats,* a list of nouns, prior to the relational propositions, twenty-seven of them. We have already noted that subjective form is both a category of existence (the fourth) and a category of explanation (the thirteenth). But must there be a thing prior to its acting on something else? Not if being is relational, and the fourth category of explanation states that every "'being' is a potential for every 'becoming.' This is the 'principle of relativity.'"

Without becoming there would be no being. The ninth category, which is restated later in *Process and Reality,* is "How an actual entity becomes constitutes *what* that actuality (or *actual* entity) is" (*PR,* 34, 252). In the context of relating the philosophy of organism and process to Hegelian categories, Whitehead adds: "This principle states that the *being* of an [actual occasion] is constituted by its 'becoming'" (*PR,* 252).

We are in need of an example of an explanation, a how, and Whitehead provides the vivid one of being angry, one example of a "subjective form," and the interpretation shows the extreme importance in metaphysics. It is not merely that a man is angry, he becomes angry because roused by some circumstance. He remains angry, not merely because he remembers, but because the later stage conforms to the earlier feeling. The anger is continuous throughout the successive occasions of experience. This continuity of subjective form is the initial sympathy of *B* for *A*. It is the primary ground for the continuity of nature (*AI,* 235–36).

Although we may answer *what* with a name, a noun stating what that is called, when we are asked *how* we must primarily use a verb to communicate a dynamic structure. Althought "feeling" is a noun when we say "a feeling," it is derived from the verb "A feeling D," and more clearly: "The 'subjective form' . . . is *how* that subject feels that objective datum" (*PR,* 338).

The process is a becom*ing,* and the verbal participial occurs in actualiz-
ing of potentials as "ingres*sion*" of forms and "objectificat*ion*" of actualities. Latin nouns with -ion endings name activities as in "act*ion*". We
have seen how important is prehens*ion* by feeling, and these may be
positive (advers*ion*) or negative (avers*ion*), and similarly there is affirmat*ion*
and negat*ion.* There is causat*ion* "efficient and final" and the eighteenth
category through the twenty-sixth category all deal with funct*ions* and
even "funct*ioning.*"

When Whitehead was a teacher of mathematics his pedagogy was based
on emphasis on a few crucial ideas. Among them he stressed an idea that
recurs in his categoreal scheme. This is "function," introduced appropriately in these last Categories of Explanation. "A function in analysis is
the counterpart of a law in the physical universe, and of a curve in
geometry" (*AE,* 89). The idea is generalized in the conceptual scheme into
the idea of how events become definite or determinate. We should
approach the categoreal scheme as he advised teachers of mathematics to
present mathematics: "The art of reasoning consists in getting hold of the
subject at the right end, of seizing on the few general ideas which
illuminate the whole, and of persistently marshaling all subsidiary facts
round them. Nobody can be a good reasoner unless by constant practice he
has realized the importance of getting hold of the big ideas and of hanging
on to them like grim death" (*AE,* 90–91).

With attention fixed on the many dynamic connections between
things, if "the task of philosophy is the understanding of the interfusion of
modes of existence" (*MT,* 97) we can account for the need of twenty-seven
categories of explanation. Probably the best development is in *Modes of
Thought,* where we read of "forms of transition" (*MT,* 112–13). Ancient
philosophers, and still some successors, think of forms as static, and
experience is the succession of forms. Whitehead illustrates this from Plato
and Hume. Whitehead's "transition" is dynamic, the forms of succession:

Today we conceive of forms of transition. The modern concept of an infinite
series is the concept of a form of transition, namely, the character of the series as a
whole is such a form. The notion of the sum of such a series is the notion of a final
issue indicated by this form of transition (*MT,* 112–13).

Only by asking "How do things function?" can we account for life and
motion (*MT,* 113). We are reminded again that Whitehead made causal
efficacy prior to presentational immediacy: the dynamic cannot be discovered in the abstract, but asymmetrically, we go by abstraction from the
dynamic to the static.

Why is transition so important? Given a universe in which we have both many and one, we may expect the transition from many to one or from one to many. This is exactly the application that makes crucial disjunction and conjunction. "Concrescence" is an instance of the advance from disjunction to conjunction. That is "the process in which the universe of many things acquires an individual unity in a determinate relegation of each item of the 'many' to its subordination in the constitution of the novel 'one'" (*PR*, 321). Thus a new concrete order emerges when the process is growth. The *crescere* of "concrescence" means "to grow," and what Whitehead's system provides is an account of growth as ordering of many into a new one.

Both disorder and order are "primary aspects of the universe" (*MT*, 71) and "there is no reason to hold that confusion is less fundamental than is order" (*MT*, 70). These are not static aspects but dynamic processes. There may be a unifying, an interconnecting, and a fulfilling of purpose, culminating in enjoyment. Or there may be the dividing that involves "conflict [and] frustration" (*MT*, 71).

The order of growth has a direction. Not only do many become one, but opposites become contrasts, so we have the notion of a more varied and richer whole.

But when we think of processes of growth, we must also consider processes of decay. Not only may many become one, but one may become many. Does the philosophy of organism recognize that, as W. B Yeats wrote, "Things fall apart, the centre cannot hold"? Whitehead, as we have seen, was acutely aware of chaos, or as the poet wrote, "sheer anarchy is loosed upon the earth." The philosopher puts it: "There is no reason to hold that confusion is less fundamental than is order" (*MT*, 70).

"Ruin" is the result of transition from contrast to opposition, from an harmonious tension to a disharmonious enmity. Whitehead illustrates how changing a color ruins a painting (*MT*, 81–82). These are evaluations. The *hows* lead us to the *whys* in which evaluations are justified.

The *Whys*: The Categoreal Obligations

In answer to a question "Why?" we most commonly answer by giving a purpose or end of the action. If the *what* is a process, with various *hows* of active functions, it is only natural that such a process should have phases. "Th[e] final phase is termed the 'satisfaction'" (*PR*, 38). This is "one complex, fully determinate feeling." Thus the categoreal scheme includes "final causation" or purpose in addition to efficient causation stressed among categories of *how* (*PR*, 36–37), as categories of *what* have included material and formal causation.

Not all ends are achieved: but whatever purpose we have is either fulfilled or frustrated. Events turn out well, or badly; persons succeed, or fail. Characteristically Whitehead uses a metaphor from the life of the sailor on the narrow seas:

A chain of facts is like a barrier reef. On one side there is wreckage, and beyond it harborage and safety. The categories governing the determination of things are the *reasons why* there should be evil, and are also the *reasons why,* in the advance of the world, particular evil facts are finally transcended. (*PR,* 341, italics added)

The importance of this passage is that it shows us the connection betweeen the most ordinary needs that demand satisfying, such as being able to step from ship to shore. There are elementary needs, such as hunger and thirst, and the humble acts of getting food and drink are under circumstances determining whether needs are or are not satisfied. At least one meaning of "good" is to be satisfied and correspondingly one meaning of "evil" is to be frustrated. Although it is often remarked that Whitehead did not develop an ethics or theory of morals, his view of the cosmos is one of values as real as the processes themselves. To ignore good and evil would be to miss something that is real. Perhaps he did not develop an ethics because so much of ethics seemed to him merely conventional. Certainly, as we have already seen, he regarded past metaphysics as "overmoralized." He laid a basis for a metaphysics of morals that did not read "thou shalt's" and "thou shalt not's" into the events. There is already life and death integral to all organisms.

The characteristic word that designates the fulfillment of aim and the accomplishment of purpose is "satisfaction" (*PR,* 39, ii, iii). Rather than obligation, which connotes moral duty and law, or even condition, which connotes situation, the third class of categories should have been called categories of "satisfaction" or of "fulfillment of aim" or of "purposes," or as we have said, to be short and colloquial, "categories of why."

The conditions under which we live induce us to ask "reasons why." These "categoreal obligations" are renamed later in *Process and Reality* (*PR,* 340) "categoreal conditions" and they "flow from the final nature of things." Although there is a list of nine, the account of three main ones stresses unity, identity and diversity. The best statement is this:

There are three main categoreal conditions which flow from the final nature of things. These three conditions are: (i) the category of subjective unity, (ii) the category of objective identity, and (iii) the category of objective diversity. . . . The three conditions . . . have an air of ultimate metaphysical generality.

The first category has to do with self-realization [the earlier statement used "integration," *PR*, 39]. Self-realization is the ultimate fact of facts. An actuality is self-realizing, and whatever is self-realizing is an actuality. An actual entity is at once the subject of self-realization, and the superject which is self-realized. (*PR*, 340).

Usually modern philosophers divorce truth and falsehood, as they do good and evil, from questions of being. But if the nature of becoming is self-realization, the achievement of identity, then the basis of logic lies in things. Is the meaning here that because a thing is what it is that we can say "if a proposition is true, then it is true"? Whitehead on this level is suggesting the traditional characterization of being as truth, and the traditional characterization of being as good. But he cannot make this full identification because it might seem to imply that whatever is, is good, and to deny the reality of frustration and failure to achieve unity balanced by diversity. The balance, similar to that between order and disorder, is the norm of excellence.

Rather than degrees of being, to square the identity of being and good, with evil toward the nothing at the lower end, as a lower degree of being, Whitehead has degrees of achievement. Thus is discovered in things the reasons why some are better and others worse. "Each actual entity . . . *attains its measure of 'order'* " (*PR*, 127). At the lower end of the scale are the actualities that do not "adapt . . . for the attainment of an end," that fail of intense satisfaction, that miss the transformation of possible incompatibilities into contrasts, and that fail as subjects to develop into "superjects" (*PR*, 127–28).

The curious neologism "superject" needs to be explained just at this point because purpose is found in a "subject-superject." Becoming has the tendency to develop in a direction, and Whitehead adopts the physical term "vector." This force going from here to there is enriched in metaphysics. The vector character (of a prehension) "involves emotion, and purpose, and valuation, and causation" (*PR*, 28). "Feelings are 'vectors'; for they feel what is *there* and transform it into what is *here*" (*PR*, 133).

The subject-superject is as self-creating as God, and as self-transcending. The best passage states the divergence from any determinism, the doctrine that creatures are what they become because acted on by external causes. It is feeling, and purposive feeling, that is the essence of each actual entity.

The term "subject" has been retained because in this sense it is familiar in philosophy. But it is misleading. The term "superject" would be better. The subject-superject is the purpose of the process originating the feelings. The feelings are inseparable from the end at which they aim; and this end is the feeler. The feelings aim at the feeler, as their final cause. The feelings are what they are in order that their subject may be what it is. Then transcendently, since the subject is what it is in virtue of its feelings, it is only by means of its feelings that the subject objectively conditions the creativity transcendent beyond itself. In our own relatively high grade of human existence, this doctrine of feelings and their subject is best illustrated by our notion of moral responsibility. The subject is responsible for being what it is in virtue of its feelings. It is also derivatively responsible for the consequences of its existence because they flow from its feelings. (PR, 339)

If the subject-predicate form of statement be taken to be metaphysically ultimate, it is then impossible to express this doctrine of feelings and their superject. It is better to say that the feelings *aim at* their subject, than to say that they *are aimed at* their subject. For the latter mode of expression removes the subject from the scope of the feeling and assigns it to an external agency. Thus the feeling would be wrongly abstracted from its final cause. This final cause is an inherent element in the feeling, constituting the unity of that feeling. An actual entity feels as it does feel in order to be the actual entity it is. In this way an actual entity satisfies Spinoza's notion of substance: it is *causa sui*. The creativity is not an external agency with its own ulterior purposes. All actual entities share with God this characteristic of self-causation. For this reason every actual entity also shares with God the characteristic of transcending all other actual entities, including God. The universe is thus a creative advance into novelty. (PR, 339–40)

This magnificent passage shows the metaphysical scheme no picture of a "static morphological universe," but of all creatures led by man in striving for the highest degree of excellence. Once again the metaphysics, as in Aristotle, becomes a theology. If we have any difficulty conceiving of a divine being, Whitehead replies, consider the nature of another free, purposive, creative, and responsible creature.

Conclusion: Canst Thou by Searching Describe the Universe?

Adverbs modify verbs, and since we have followed Whitehead's attention to the *whats, hows,* and *whys,* renaming his three groups of categories that modify creativity, creativity itself should be renamed. A noun is inadequate because definite and static. Whitehead does use the Latin *creare,* "to bring forth, beget, produce" (*PR,* 324). Just as St. Thomas Aquinas characterized being itself as *esse,* and English-speaking Thomists say of God, "the to be," or "the act of being," so we might rethink Whitehead and say, "the to produce" and keep the dynamism that only verbs express with a degree of adequacy. The participial *be-ing* is better than the noun *being.* Whitehead's system is one of becoming if, and only if, we specify some precise ways of becoming, or the forms of transition. Probably we should make the *hows* prior to the *whats* (and add *whiches* and *whos*), and make plain that the dynamism expressed adverbially is in *whithers* and *whences* more than *wheres* and *whens.* There is a vector character of becoming. The *whys* are continuous with the *hows* and *whats,* and the usage of the iterrogative *how?* sometimes means *why?* And *what?* also sometimes means *why?* Although we have not detailed the eight categories of existence, twenty-seven categories of explanation, and nine categorial obligations (or conditions), we have done something much needed while reading Whitehead; this is to respond imaginatively to an imaginative metaphysician.

It is a deeper faithfulness to the spirit of Whitehead to interpret him creatively than to restate him literally. He meant his "system" to be one of many, and one which could inspire other categoreal schemes, among which, he had no doubt, some would be more adequate to experience. There is no reason to think there is anything sacred about $3 + 8 + 27 + 9 = 47$. He had a rather large number of categories, when compared with the traditional ten pairs from Pythagoras, then ten of Aristotle—yet Hegel is sometimes credited with hundreds (272), and contemporary analytic philosophers tell us there are as many as each speaker cares to distinguish.[7]

Since there is no reason to think the "Categoreal Scheme" of *Process and Reality* the only possible set of categories, and since in that work from its initial statement no more than a few parts recur, and *Adventures of Ideas* and *Modes of Thought,* subsequent to it, do not use it, we should feel quite free to explore alternatives. If categoreal thinking is about the ordering of things, one way to adapt Whitehead is to think of the orders we need to distinguish. That is the method of this book.

Whitehead discusses categories of a system under "Adventure." He states that Plato largely escaped the static notion, "deceived by the beauty of mathematics intelligible in unchanging perfection, conceived of a super-world of ideas, forever perfect and forever interwoven" (*AI,* 354). The alternative is that the "very essence of real actuality—that is, of the completely real—is *process*" (*AI,* 354). Plato's "later Dialogues circle round seven notions, namely—The Ideas, The Physical Elements, The

Psyche, The Eros, The Harmony, The Mathematical Relations, The Receptacle."[8] If Whitehead means that "all philosophy is in fact an endeavor to obtain a coherent system out of some modifications of these notions," then the essence of Whitehead's categoreal scheme is a reinterpretation of Plato. We should ask whether he did enough in stressing Psyche (Soul) and Eros, "the urge towards the realization of ideal perfection" (*AI,* 354). Without these "we should obtain a static world. The 'life and motion,' which are essentials in Plato's later thought, are derived from the operation of these two factors. But Plato left no system of metaphysics" (*AI,* 355; cf. a comparable list of twelve categories from Descartes and Locke, (*PR,* 196). Why, then, if we can do metaphysics without a system or without a categoreal scheme, should we not reject Aristotle and follow Plato?

Whitehead is well aware that his many categories will strike the reader as muddled. Why not be clear? Newton had clarity about "four types of entities. . . . for him minds are actual things, bodies are actual things, absolute durations of time are actual things, and absolute places are actual things" (*PR,* 111). All are on the same level as matter of fact. "The result is to land him in a clearly expressed but complex and arbitrary scheme of relations between spaces *inter se.* Like most simple common sense answers, Newton's is "simple, plausible, and wrong" (*PR,* 111). The fundamental Whiteheadian argument about any categoreal scheme is that since it is not a simple world, no simple system can be adequate (*RM,* 76, 71).

Along with a final justification of metaphysical system there comes again, at the end, a warning, as at the beginning of the enterprise.

Philosophic systems with their ambitious aims at full comprehensiveness, are not useless. They are the way in which the human spirit cultivates its deeper intuitions. Such systems give life and motion to detached thoughts. Apart from these efforts at coordination, detached thoughts would flash out in idle moments, illuminate a passing phase of reflection, and would then perish and be forgotten. The scope of an intuition can only be defined by its coordination with other notions of equal generality. (*AI,* 184–85)

The failure is to appreciate the fact that "competing philosophic systems are . . . essential for progress." In medieval theology and among modern scientists, in Whitehead's judgment, is "the persuasion that we are capable of producing notions which are adequately defined" for the complex relations of reality. This is the Dogmatic Fallacy.

The error consists in the persuasion that we are capable of producing notions adequate [to] . . . the real world. Canst thou by searching describe the Universe? (*AI*, 185)

Once again we have a deep reflection of biblical wisdom. Jehovah rebukes Job: "Canst thou by searching find out God?" (Job 11:7). In his interpretation of the text Whitehead is a bold Greek as against a humble Hebrew. But in his reflection on the boldest of Greek sciences, metaphysics, he shows the humility of the faithful Hebrew rebuking the proud Greek: "Canst thou by searching describe the Universe?" (*AI*, 185).

Chapter Seven

The Vision of Order and the Saving Order: The Antecedent and Consequent Natures of God

Introduction

It is sometimes said that Whitehead, because he was essentially a religious man, had to develop a religious philosophy. It is true, and existentially important, that he was the son of an Anglican priest, but it is no less relevant to his philosophy that his father was also a schoolmaster, and also that Whitehead lived a rich married life with his wife, who loved the arts, and that his greatest student was a fellow logician, Bertrand Russell. Among the great concerns of human culture Whitehead cared about all of them, history as well as mathematics, physics as well as metaphysics. Probably because he was brought up with family ties to Anglican Christianity it was easier for him to respond deeply to Platonism, a philosophy which had flourished two centuries earlier in Cambridge, his university, but this commitment also made him more deeply sensitive to the intellectual decline and social complacency of the Established Church of England.[1] His writings show sympathy with George Fox and other Quaker critics of the Church, and with John Wesley and other Methodists whose concerns had been to awaken the Church to the problems of the neglected poor of a newly industrialized society.

Whitehead is one of many Victorians who struggled between the alternatives of continuing in the genial orthodoxy of his Anglican father and grandfather, or becoming, with his wife, Roman Catholic. Neither alternative seemed intellectually satisfying: one was superficial and the other restrictively and oppressively dogmatic (the time was the turn of the century, when scriptural scholars were persecuted as "modernists"). Twenty years of agnosticism and barely relieved indifference were broken, to the great surprise of his philosophic acquaintances, by the chapter "God" in *Science and the Modern World*. His great colleague and friend Russell wrote a review, "Is Science Superstitious?"

Why did Whitehead find it necessary, in his writings between 1925 and 1933, to rethink the whole problem of religion and God, and why was he able to do so? The best simple answer is that his entire career as a mathematician, logician, and philosopher of science had been devoted to the study of order. Science itself, we saw above, presupposed that nature is an intelligible order.

There is every evidence that Whitehead, in his own case with regard to the Western tradition, acknowledges that he was dependent on biblical faith. "In the beginning God created the heaven and the earth. And the earth was without form and void; and darkness was upon the face of the deep. And the Spirit of God moved upon the face of the waters. And God said Let there be light: and there was light" (Genesis 1:1–3). The creation story, taken as Newton took it, led the physicist to seek the laws which Jehovah had impressed upon matter. Although Newton's God, as Newton's physics, became for Whitehead a hypothetical and a partial truth, the association of God with order remained a necessary or defining relationship of both (*AI,* 45–46).

If science discovers order and religion puts faith in order, what is the relation? Since Whitehead was dissatisfied with the easy lay answer that science proves God or the easy theological answer that there are proofs of God's existence, it was a necessity for him to examine religions and their distinctive claims. "Religion is the reaction of human nature to its search for God" (*SMW,* 274).

The major religions of mankind all affirm that man inhabits a cosmos, and in nearly all the great myths it is God Who is the majestic agency Who has brought *cosmos out of chaos*. It has been ever perplexing to mankind, once it has achieved philosophy and science and an historical and anthropological understanding of the variety of myths, whether the traditions can be given any credence, and, if they can, how their truth may be restated. Whitehead is one who revised the myth. He sought a metaphysics that could admit God. Or should we say that he sought a metaphysical statement that God is required?

Although we have detailed the categoreal scheme of *whats, hows,* and *whys* first, it might fairly be objected that the deep root of metaphysics is in myth, and that we should first consider the ageold questions about the *whence* and *whither* of man and the cosmos. For is there not in the metaphysician's heart, prior to considering any scheme, the conviction that all that happens belongs together intelligibly? The conviction is clear in Whitehead that sheer chaos (absolute absence of all order, not disorder) is intrinsically impossible. (Chaos is called "an ideal zero" [*PR,* 176].)

The scheme allows the highly heretical physicist and metaphysician to be rather orthodox: some majestic something secured order out of chaos, and prevents its return to chaos (*AI,* 132). Of course it would not be proper to say "God" unless this agency were regarded as the source of good, enjoyed as manifested, and the ground of hope. Whitehead's writings about God have a note of gratitude and hope that have been welcome to religious philosophers as akin to worship. It must be added that those hostile to religion have found it an expression of "disgusting uplift."

The climax of Whitehead's metaphysics is his doctrine of the cosmic opposites, God and the world. This is by far the most readable part of *Process and Reality* and is easily comprehensible to anyone who enjoys his popular *Religion in the Making,* and the chapter "God" in *Science and the Modern World,* together with various other chapters on the problem of religious faith and such other claims to truth, as those of the sciences. Together these contributions have made Whitehead a major philosopher of religion, and a defender of his own version of philosophical theology and of a rational religion comparable to those of Plato, Plotinus, the Upanishads, Maimonides, and Spinoza. Undoubtedly the great bulk of "Whitehead-ians," among whom the chief is Charles Hartshorne, are those deeply impressed by the ability of the categories of the system to reinterpret the religious heritage of mankind, particularly to give a new theory of God, a theory based on rejection of all the old proofs of a God wholly transcendent.

The contribution is a remarkable expansion of philosophy and it has attracted world-wide attention. It must not be thought that Whitehead, although some of his writings are addressed to Protestant audiences, has failed to be attractive to Catholics. The contrary is the case. There is a process theology of Catholics, notably that of Ewert Cousins, linking Whitehead with St. Bonaventura.[2] Also because Whitehead broadened his base by attention to far Eastern cultures, particularly Buddhism, *Religion in the Making* is Whitehead's bid to be considered a world philosopher. It is quite possible to be a Buddhist Whiteheadian, and there are eminent examples.

Whitehead is no positivist who thinks that empirical sciences have rendered theology obsolete. A metaphysician, as against a positivist, keeps the priority of "*What* do we know?" to "*How* do we know?" (*AI*, 159) and the "what" may include God. Whitehead accepts some religious teachings as true and rejects others as false, just as he considers some religious practices as barbarous in contrast to others which are productive of high civilization. To outline this discrimination we need to take account of religion in history (§ 2); criticism of religious teachings (§ 3); the metaphysical problem of the *whence* and *whither* (§ 4); the two natures of God: antecedent and consequent (§ 5); creation and entropy: order out of chaos, or chaos out of order (§ 6)?

Religion in History: Has There Been and Can There Be Progress?

Whitehead's approach to religion is historical. It is part of his approach to civilization, ideas, and science, and *Religion in the Making* is, as he says, one side of a general picture, along with *Process and Reality, Science and the Modern World, Adventures of Ideas* (*RM*, 7, *AI*, vii). Every title presupposes the importance of time and change: "Making," "Process," "Modern," "Adventures." "Historical does *not* mean love of the past and disparise of the present." Why should religion be approached historically? Whitehead appeals to the Bible, in which the Hebrew prophets, priests, and kings play a special role, and Whitehead accepts it as a most progressive one significant for all humanity (*AI*, Part 1). But also through history we learn of other founders, such as Mohammed and Gotama Buddha. Without history we should not have access to them as to the inspiration of Jesus. If the quality of experience of the saints is unique and rare, no psychology and sociology of ordinary people would give us any idea of how world religions began and continue to guide civilization. As the rabbis said of Moses Maimonides, "From Moses to Moses (Maimonides) there was none like unto Moses." Only an historical approach enables us to trace the influences of the inspiration of the founders on civilization generally, including the arts, sciences, and philosophy. To the extent that meaning lies in consequences, to tear religions out of history is to rob them of significance. As we saw in Whitehead's philosophy of civilization, ideas are capable of progress, and Whitehead is counteracting the secularist notions that religions are archaic nuisances inconsistent with the most advanced of modern cultures. Without religious inspiration, how could there be the civilizations named according to the guiding faiths? In future time further advance hinges on how Hindus, Buddhists, Taoists, and Confucians together with Western religions shape a rational religion of all mankind. The knowledge of the past is to improve the future. *Adventures of Ideas* attributes the decline of civilization to decay of religion. ". . . There stands the inexorable law that apart from some transcendent aim the civilized life either wallows in pleasure or relapses slowly into a barren repetition with waning intensities of feeling" (*AI*, 108). This is also the major theme of Arnold Toynbee's *Study of History*.[3] From Whitehead's perspective, the essence of education is to be religious, and an irreligious education would neglect duty and reverence (*AE*, 26). These are other words for "transcendent aim" and this is an apt philosophic description of the express purposes of all the great founders. There is a strong sense in which Whitehead is writing prophetic history.

When we say that Whitehead's approach is "historical" we do not mean, then, that he gathered data to give a full account of any specific event. He had a command of fact that astonished his friends because he knew the exact dates of great figures, and he knew their writings, particularly letters, which he trusted to reveal how people of the past thought and felt. The primary sense in which Whitehead is "historical" is the sense in which Hegel was "historical": creating a general picture of significance in the stages of progress. In Whitehead's case, as in Hegel's, neither the accuracy of fact, usually very good in Whitehead's case, but usually very bad in Hegel's case, confirms or disconfirms the philosophical history. ". . . Our history of ideas is derivative from our ideas of history" (*AI*, 8; an alternative to any idea of "pure history" devoid of prejudice or principles, a "figment of the imagination": *AI*, 4).

The complex of "religion," incapable of simple definition, though Whitehead offers half a dozen statements beginning "religion is . . . ," is analyzed into "four factors or sides of itself. These factors are ritual, emotion, belief, rationalization" (*RM*, 18). The obvious reason for beginning with ritual is that "definite organized procedure[s]" are recognized among animals as well as significantly among humans in repetitive actions that characterized the arts, combined with play and sport (*RM*, 20–22). Collective emotions are stimulated by rituals and help bind a society together (*RM*, 22–23). Of beliefs and rationalization we shall have more below because they are of greater importance. "The order of the emergence of these factors was in the inverse order of the depth of their religious importance: first ritual, then emotion, then belief, then rationalization" (*RM*, 18–19).

What is meant by "depth" of experience? This is the norm by which Jesus Christ and Gotama Buddha stand out as the great religious figures in the whole history of mankind. Jesus was, like Hebrew prophets before

him, highly independent of popular cult. Gotama was, like seers of
Hinduism, primarily stating a set of metaphysical principles. We recognize the contrast between one who was intimate with God as Father and
one who was officially agnostic. Yet the gospel of God as Love, proclaimed
by the man on the cross, and the Gospel of release from suffering and
universal compassion, had, as no other religious messages, the greatest
universal appeal. So much is historic fact. Whitehead adds an interpretation of the historical situation that the highest genius in religion is this
freedom from tribal constraints, and the freedom for the statement of
general truths that can apply to all mankind. The Gospel of Christ
converted Gentiles and the Gospel of Buddha the Southeastern Asians,
Chinese, Koreans, and Japanese. "Religion" in these examples "is what an
individual does with his own solitariness" (*RM*, 16). Whitehead recognizes the deep differences between the Christian intensification of personality, with hope of immortal life with God, and the Buddhist denial of
desire and release from karma and enjoyment of nirvana (*RM*, 40, 44,
49–52) but very skillfully Whitehead states what can be true of both:
"Religion is the art and the theory of the internal life of man, so far as it
depends on the man himself and on what is permanent in the nature of
things" (*RM*, 16). Neither Jesus nor Buddha deceived his followers about
the importance of evil in human experience, and this is essential to an
honest philosophy, and a great contribution of religion to philosophy.
Curiously Whitehead neglects the Christian rebuke to sin and the Buddhist depreciation of desire, since obviously these are what need to be
cleansed. Whitehead as metaphysician recognized the metaphysical clarity
of the Buddhist doctrine of "escape" (*RM*, 50–51). Whitehead as a
Christian recognized the Judaic genius of Christianity, its concentration
on facts, often of the lowest level of generality (*RM*, 51). Therefore
Christianity is "a religion seeking a metaphysic, in contrast to Buddhism
which is a metaphysic generating a religion" (*RM*, 50). What is meant by
"fact" is significant. Whitehead is quite typical of the liberal historical
method of selecting from the Gospels what is called the "Gospel of Jesus"
and ignoring the "Gospel about Jesus." That is, as a rationalist, he ignored
completely what Christian creeds are about, the incarnation of God
through a virgin, the sacrifice on the cross, and the bodily resurrection of
Jesus. What is significant? "In the Sermon on the Mount, in the Parables,
and in their accounts of Christ, the Gospels exhibit a tremendous fact"
(*RM*, 51). What then did Whitehead think of the miracles? Probably,
since he praises Hume's *Dialogues Concerning Natural Religion* so very
highly, and indeed wanted to be yet another speaker in that masterpiece

(*PR*, 521) he dismissed them as ignorant and incredible, and even worse, a corrupting of the message. Similarly, he chose to ignore the considerable emphasis in the Gospels on the condemnation of the wicked and sinful to the flames of eternal damnation. We know how revolted he felt by the images of hellfire in the last book of the New Testament, the Revelation of St. John the Divine, the Apocalypse; this he wished expunged, and in its place substituted the oration of Pericles (*AI*, 219).

There are numerous other ways in which Whitehead argues for the Hellenic version of Christianity as superior, and a critical interpretation should recognize that many scholars would argue the contrary.

Although *Religion in the Making* is richly empirical, allowing a place for psychology insofar as religion takes place within a person, anthropology insofar as religion occurs between persons in a culture, history insofar as there are religious institutions, religion is most important as a claim to the truth about the cosmos. Whitehead is concerned with the kind of religion that can survive in an age of science. When religion is stated as belief, then only can it be considered in relation to facts, and continued because true. (*SMW*, 259–76; *AI*, 205–21).

Since alternative cosmologies are being discussed, there can be no adequate status of religion in the modern world without metaphysics. The problem is "the foundation . . . on our apprehension of those permanent elements by reason of which there is a stable order in the world, permanent elements apart from which there could be no changing world" (*RM*, vii). This follows from the importance of belief, and the impossibility of ignoring science. Science suggests a cosmology, and whatever suggests a cosmology suggests a religion.

Although we began saying that "Whitehead's approach to religion is historical," when we examine the meaning of "historical" we find this is essentially "metaphysical." Although Whitehead was indebted to the historical approach of the nineteenth century that gives us the broad view of all religions, each approached from its own perspective, he deplores such "dominance of the historical interest" that would exclude metaphysics. "It is a curious delusion that the rock upon which our beliefs can be founded is an historical investigation." Although science may ignore explicit metaphysics, religion longs for "justification of belief, and this cannot be naive faith, and the great "ages of faith are the ages of rationalism" (*RM*, 85–86, a point made explicit in *Science and the Modern World* 83). The criticism of belief rests on a "rational metaphysics which criticizes meanings, and endeavors to express the most general concepts adequate for the all-inclusive universe" (*RM,* 83). These principles can be found only in the present and "you can only interpret the past in terms of the present."

Yet if we should grant the claim that religions are fundamentally metaphysical, and concern the nature of God, then the problem arises of whether the concept is true and good. The three rough ways of characterizing God are as indifferent (or neutral), as hostile, and as cooperative. Whitehead has no doubt that the transition is progress. There are three stages of the process, "It is the transition from God the void to God the enemy, and from God the enemy to God the companion" (*RM,* 16–17).

Whitehead does not amplify his most succinct statement, therefore requiring us to interpret it. Among very many suggestions, this is here the most appropriate. In the beginning there seems to be chaos because we cannot find intelligible order. Then we ascribe law to power that has imposed order. But finally we find order in the events in which we participate, an ordering of the events by agents themselves. This myth of progress is of stages from force to persuasion. An enemy may force us to act according to his will, but a friend would persuade us to act according to reason in which we both share.

Whitehead's great poetic gift was in creating a myth which readers may use imaginatively. It links human significance with the cosmos. Some now say that the "death of God" movement signifies a transition from God the friend to God the enemy, and from God the enemy to God the void. Whitehead not only denies the death but proclaims in us a rebirth.

Criticism of Religions: Meanings of "Truth"

"Truth" is as ambiguous as "religion" and the combination, as in "religious truth," is almost beyond calculation. Yet we have a theory of factors and stages of religion that gives us some clarity. Does *Religion in the Making* help us also with regard to the meanings of truth? Part of the difficulty is that modern philosophy has tended to reduce the meanings of truth to truth-of-fact or truth-of-logic, as in the contrast between "this pencil is yellow" and "yellow is yellow." Then we may add, as we have seen Whitehead do, a pragmatic truth, as when a belief is tested by the results of acting upon it. We are then led to the attempt to sort out claims as to whether they are empirical or conceptual or pragmatic. Whitehead, of all great twentieth-century philosophers, is open to an integration of the special theories of truth because each is too narrow alone and needs to be criticized and amplified (*AI,* Chapter 16). He broadens "truth" to include metaphorical statement and emotional import, without however reducing religious truth to myth and symbol or to emotion.

"There is no agreement as to . . . true and false religion; nor . . . even to what we mean by truth of religion" (RM, 14). Why does not Whitehead apply his theory of truth to the philosophy of religion? Although we might give an empirical, a logical, or a pragmatic meaning to the truth of 69×67, and know what we mean by the true answer to the question of their product, the truth of religion is elusive. Whereas "you *use* arithemetic, . . . you *are* religious" (RM, 15). "This is the primary religious truth from which no one can escape. Religion is the force of belief cleansing the inward parts. For this reason the primary religious virtue is sincerity, a penetrating sincerity" (RM, 15). Now if this were the only meaning of "truth" in religion, then we could say that we need only add to the three standard philosophic meanings a fourth, which might be called personal truthfulness. But it is obviously not the only meaning of "truth" in religion, for there is also what is affirmed in doctrine of a faith, sometimes stated in a creed. There is "a system of general truths," and here we have theology, similar to metaphysics, and "truth" here is not merely empirical, or logical, or pragmatic, or a matter of personal sincerity.

The best approach to Whitehead's contribution to the problem of religious truth is to follow the Oxford English Dictionary definitions of "true" and "truth," preferably in the unabridged edition, which have fourteen meanings. Number one is the quality of a person, "faithfulness, good faith, loyalty; honesty."[4] This is in the archaic language of the traditional English marriage service "troth," as in "I plight thee my troth," and with this Whitehead begins: he calls it "sincerity." The advantage of beginning with the most primitive meaning historically is that it is an attitude prior to an act or a statement. The second meaning flows from it, the act of making a promise or of entering into a covenant. Out of this we make a transition to "faith, trust, confidence" and "religious belief" in the form of a "creed."

It is unnecessarily tedious to run through fourteen meanings of "truth" and to examine whether Whitehead's analysis of religion requires that all of them be recognized and illustrated. All that is needed, beyond beginning with the person's sincerity and his or her "disposition to speak or act truly or without deceit," is to consider the agreement of what is believed with reality, whether in particular events or in general structure, and then to develop the ways in which religious truth is claimed to be identical with that reality.

What is important is not so much the number of meanings of "truth" in religion as the range of meanings. They run from the most subjective to the most objective. In the former, the opposite of "true," which means "faithful," is "dishonest," while at the extreme of objectivity where truth is identical with fact, the opposite is "illusion." Whitehead goes this far in his belief in order. "Chaos" is an ideal nothing. The great instance of sufficient objectivity to judge that a religious proposition is false is illustrated by the problem of evil.

The false can emerge in religion only when a belief is formulated clearly enough to be tested experientially. One of the risks taken by religion when it claims that a belief can be verified or shown to be true to the facts is that it may be disconfirmed or shown to be false. A possible dogma about the nature of God is that His power is absolute, that God is omnipotent. When this is coupled with the dogma that God is also all knowing and all just, we have omnipotence coupled with omniscience and omnibenevolence. These assumptions were developed, Whitehead shows, in Hebrew religious thought. The logical conclusion is that the world ruled by God must be perfectly just. One application is that there is no unmerited suffering, or that only the wicked are unhappy, or that all suffering is punishment for sin. Is it then the "best of all possible worlds" because "the justice of God is beautifully evident in everything that happens" (*RM*, 48)?

The assumptions together produce the falsehood evident to Job. It is in the Bible that the sophism is considered: if a man suffers, then he must have sinned. It is the triumph of religious rationalism to tear the sophism to shreds. If one keeps omniscience and omnibenevolence, then what is dispensable in the attributes of God is omnipotence, especially in the concept of tyrannical power. That is, it is unwarranted to ascribe every act in the world to the single agent God. The interesting use of the Book of Job by Whitehead is that it establishes one truth about God from within religious thought: to maintain God's goodness and wisdom, the attribute of omnipotence must be abandoned. It must be noted that upon discovering the inconsistency of this definition of God with the facts of moral experience, some philosophers conclude that God therefore does not exist or cannot be known to exist. Rather than a destructive conclusion, Whitehead takes a constructive path. What is needed is a reconceptualization of God.

Job's "rational criticism" is of the "old-fashioned tribal God" and opens the way for another sort of "rationalism" (*RM*, 48–49). This is the use of direct intuition in the teachings of Jesus (*RM*, 56–57). Whitehead's method is to recognize the importance of argument, but not to follow the lead of the medievals who felt that they had first to demonstrate the existence of God (*SMW*, 83). The way of intuition is not so much trust in the principle of contradiction as a search for the ground of such a formulation. "It cannot be true that contradictory notions can apply to the same fact" (*RM*, 77). This must apply to God, not both *p* and -*p*. Therefore in divorcing religious discourse from dialectics, he does not fall into irrationalism. The ground of metaphysical rationalism is a direct grasp of "rightness" (*RM*, 41, 60, 63, 66, 126, 173). It might be wondered that Whitehead appeals to something so vague and indefinite. The reason probably is that the clear intuitions as to the relation between God and the world are contradictory and there is the opportunity, as with the problem of evil, to make a fresh start (*RM*, 68–70). If there is a new basis discovered, then religious thought can get beyond the deadlocked rival claims to the transcendence or the exclusive immanence of God (*RM*, 71–72).

Whitehead's rationalism is based on the conviction that the past error is to suppose that truth must be simple. Because all the simple solutions have broken down, we now have the opportunity of "complexity of interrelations." As in physics, so in metaphysics, especially in philosophical theology (*RM*, 76).

The apprehension of "rightness of things, partly conformed to and partially disregarded" is a matter of "large consensus" (*RM*, 66). There are several examples. One is that in one moment we grasp "the value of an individual for itself," "the value of diverse individuals of the world for each other," and the value of the interrelated components of the world (*RM*, 59). This is not a traditional argument for God but a statement of religious experience. What is then said of God, that he is a Person who reveals his purpose, is then an inference, and not directly known (*RM*, 62–63).

The problem of evil then springs from the overmoralization of value, or considering all value moral value. If beauty is more basic than goodness, then a broader conception of the ultimate is attained. Earlier we heard of the "aesthetic harmony [that] stands before [the world] as a living ideal" (*SMW*, 28),

All order is . . . aesthetic order and the moral order is merely certain aspects of aesthetic order. The actual world is the outcome of the aesthetic order, and the aesthetic order is derived from the immanence of God. (*RM*, 105)

On this basis can we derive a valid metaphysical answer to the ageold religious questions of the *whence* and the *whither?*

The Metaphysical Problem of the *Whence* and the *Whither*

Religions raise most interesting questions about the cosmos and man. These are notably about the *whence* and the *whither.* By these adverbs we mean such myths of origin as creation stories and such myths of destiny as stories of transmigration, last judgment, heaven and hell, etc. The anthropomorphic answers are naive, but the questions have not been fully answered by such a conceptual scheme as that of the *whats,* the *hows,* and the *whys,* as we have so far examined in the previous chapters. At many points the "order of the system" seemed to "require" God. In spite of all the contradictions among the great faiths of mankind, there are underlying questions. If there is a cosmos, how account for the order? If the process is one of achievement, is there any preservation of value? A metaphysician might ask these questions quite independently of religion. But then some systems ignore these dimensions of reality as though the problem of God did not pose significant questions. Whitehead's method and categoreal scheme cannot consistently remain indifferent.

What must be emphasized in Whitehead's consideration of metaphysics is that religion is not all archaic nuisance to be cleared away as rubbish, but in part a tremendous stimulus to speculation. It is not only questions, such as the whence and the whither, it is certain experiences in which Whitehead trusts. And why indeed should not everyone trust a kind of experience that is as universal as any other kind? In all these, aesthetic, moral, scientific, there must be discrimination between careful, responsible, and sometimes insightful description and the contrary. There are, writes Whitehead, in religion "great standard experiences." Do these "lead to a more definite knowledge than can be derived from a metaphysic which founds itself upon general experience" (*RM,* 149)?

There is no possibility of being present at the creation or the last judgment, or trusting revelation to give accounts as though their authors had been there. It is not only skeptical philosophers who would agree with Whitehead here. So also would St. Augustine (*Confessions,* Book 12). All there can be as a foundation is a "direct intuition into the ultimate character of the universe" (*RM,* 59). If we do grasp "a principle determining the grading of values," then we can test this by coherence with the rest of our systematic understanding of the cosmos (*RM,* 59–60).

Whitehead is trying to capture in words a principle that is felt. "This principle is not a dogmatic formulation, but the intuition of immediate occasions as failing or succeeding in reference to the ideal relevant to them. *There is a rightness attained or missed,* with more or less completeness of attainment or omission" (*RM,* 60–61, italics added). Whitehead offers no examples, probably because he thinks each reader knows when doing anything, when it is bungled, or when it is perfect, etc.

The experience is closely related to that of order-disorder. "It is *a character of permanent rightness,* whose inherence in the nature of things modifies both efficient and final causes, so that the one conforms to harmonious conditions, and the other contrasts itself with an harmonious ideal. The harmony in the actual world is in conformity with the character" (*RM,* 61, italics added).

We have previously discussed the many kinds of harmony, particularly those of the Pythagorean tradition and the way Whitehead's philosophy of civilization develops this as a norm. "In some form or other all attempts to formulate the doctrines of a rational religion in ancient Greece took their stand upon the Pythagorean notion of a *direct intuition of a righteousness* in the nature of things, functioning as a condition, a critic, and an ideal" (*RM,* 63, emphasis mine). Why the shift from "rightness" to "righteousness"? It may show the importance of the morally right in addition to the logically right, aesthetically right, etc. The Greeks said *dikē.*

Whitehead appeals to India and China as well as to Greece, and here he probably means ṛta, the principle of the Vedas governing gods as well as men, the *tao t'ien* ("way of heaven") to which emperors must conform in the Confucian order, the Tao, the Way of Taoism, etc. (*RM,* 62).[5]

Is this something more general than the famous Platonic triad, Truth, Beauty, and Goodness? Exactly how is rightness related to the "harmony of logic [which] lies upon the universe as an iron necessity"? While the "aesthetic harmony stands before it as a living ideal"? This needs to be worked out (*SMW,* 28). Evidently, when "wisdom" replaces rightness, it has the practical moral meaning of "righteousness." "The final principle of religion is that there is a wisdom in the nature of things, from which flow our direction of practice, and our possibility of the theoretical analysis of fact" (*RM,* 143).

The affirmation of God is then tantamount to saying that all creation is intelligible, and this undergirds our search for truth. Just as important is the apprehension of value, aesthetic and moral. In other words: whatever is, has value, and if something has no value, it cannot be. Is God the highest intensity of value? This would be a version of the familiar

Platonistic theory that God is apprehended as the Truth in all truths, the Goodness in all good things, the Beauty in all beauties. This is a crucial problem for the steps between the ordinary actualities of the world and God. In one all-too-brief reference to the quality of every fact there is the further step that "there is still . . . the quality of the quality." What is to be made of the religious claim to apprehend that which *"contributes its quality as an immortal fact to the order which informs the world".?* (RM, 80, italics added). This is one way to rationalize the assertion of a *whence* and *whither* together.

. . . The purpose of God in the attainment of value is in a sense a creative purpose. Apart from God, the remaining formative elements would fail in their functions. There would be no creatures, since, apart from harmonious order, the perceptive fusion would be confusion, neutralizing achieved feeling. Here "feeling" is used as a synonym for "actuality." (RM, 104)

This philosophical theology stands or falls in its position on evil. One of the great contributions of religions is to call our attention to suffering, death, destruction, and the utter loss of all value. Whitehead's position steers a course between the complaining pessimism of Job and the bland optimisim of Leibniz. There is no denying real evil in pain, physical and mental, and no ignoring of conflict or "things at cross purposes" (RM, 95–97). In terms of value, there is "the loss of the higher experience in favor of the lower experience" (RM, 95). This is a shift away from identifying moral evil as sin, or the deliberate disobedience of divine command. Because of this shift away from the view of God as lawgiver and judge, there can be no such problem as that of Job and his comforters. The position is consonant to the mediating position between pessimism and optimism. William James called it "meliorism" and summed it up: "evil is good—to overcome."

"Good" in the philosophy of organism is rather like an organism's adjusting to the environment. "There is a self-preservation inherent in that which is good in itself" (RM, 98). Yet this is but one aspect, for the full nature of good must be characterized as a structure of opposites in harmony, beauty as well as truth, adventure as well as peace (AI, Part 4, pp. 309–81). Evil is one of the opposites, in the process, generally characterized as destructiveness "in contrast to the creativeness of what can without qualification be termed good." Thereby Whitehead avoids saying that evil is nothing: "Evil is positive and destructive; what is good is positive and creative" (RM, 96). In organic process the two are tendencies that are concurrent.

The only ground of meliorism must then be that when there is a tendency toward nothing, this encourages a counter tendency. The realization of evil produces its elimination. "The purpose is to secure the avoidance of evil. The fact of the instability of evil is the moral order of the world" (*RM,* 95).

By no means does this view conclude that all evil, such as suffering, is good. The individual member may "lose the delicacy of perception which results [from] that pain," and the whole species may cease. The only hope is that there is a possibility to "develop a finer and more subtle relationship among its bodily parts" (*RM,* 96).

Beyond this, Whitehead turns to God, and we must ask whether God cares about the evil and suffering. So far, there is hope only for the survivors who are well adjusted.

The Antecedent and Consequent Natures of God

The religious quest for the *whence* leads to the vision of all possibles ever with the world. The religious quest for the *whither* leads to the kingdom of God ever in and from the world. The religious quest of Plato led to the vision. The religious quest of Jesus led to the kingdom. We may take Whitehead at his word that the theory of two natures of God is the result of dispassionate inquiry (*PR,* 521) or we may say that he was harmonizing Greek and Hebrew wisdom, or even within Christian symbolism, thinking of God as Alpha and Omega, "the beginning and the end" (Rev. 21:6). Whitehead greatly admired Christian Platonism and asked, "Can there be any doubt that the power of Christianity lies in its revelation in act, of that which Plato divined in theory?" (*AI,* 214, with an elaborate claim that Alexandrian theologians improved upon Plato). There are some who regard Whitehead as one of the Cambridge Platonists, and esteem him as the last and greatest of the movement originating from the seventeenth century. Historically Whitehead can agree with Hume that the traditional concept of God and the "proofs" are untenable, but this theism is the idolatry of thinking of God as an "unmoved mover" (Aristotle) or a "personification of moral energy" (the Prophets) or "the image of an imperial ruler" (the Church of the Empire). All these should be rejected, but they leave the idea of God of "the great formative period of theistic philosophy" (*PR,* 519–20). This is the religion of Jesus, the Galilean emphasis on the love of God and the kingdom of God. Whitehead as a philosopher stresses the divine persuasion, following Plato, and therefore can accept the Gospel:

It does not emphasize the ruling Caesar, or the ruthless moralist, or the unmoved mover. It dwells on the tender elements in the world, which slowly and in quietness operate by love; and it finds purpose in the present immediacy of a kingdom not of this world. Love neither rules, nor is unmoved; also it is a little oblivious as to morals. It does not look to the future; for it finds its own reward in the immediate present. (*PR*, 520–21)

Part 5 is the "final interpretation" of the categoreal system, and it rests significantly upon such ideal opposites as stressed in all the preceding chapters: order and disorder. Order alone stifles imagination. Disorder alone is meaningless confusion. The right balance between them ensures life and progress. "The art of progress is to preserve order amid change, and to preserve change amid order" (*PR*, 515). Order alone is closely connected to permanence, and disorder alone to flux. This is "the complete problem of metaphysics," and the inadequacies of either substance alone or flux alone, or to separate the two, as Plato tended to do, loses the insight of "one integral experience" (*PR*, 318). In the end, it is images or metaphors which express "ultimate feeling" and preserve metaphysics from "thinness" (ibid.).

The argument is that all direct experience is of a world of opposites, and the dipolar principle is that we cannot have one without the other. There are endless examples other than order-disorder and permanence-flux. These are used to interpret the world, the world and God, and God. "God is not . . . an exception to all metaphysical principles, invoked to save their collapse [but] is their chief exemplification" (*PR*, 521). God, as the world, therefore, is dipolar.

Therefore, God must have two sides or two poles, the antecedent and the consequent nature. The two poles are the conceptual and the physical. God without a world would be only a vision of possibles, the eternal objects. A world without God, hardly a world at all, would have no aims or everlastingness. God and the world need each other and would be incomplete without one another. Only in this way can a timeless element be implanted in passing flux, and actualities escape into everlastingness. "They perish and are laid to rest."

The argument rests upon analogy and employs many metaphors, some familiar and some Whitehead's original religious insights. The most famous is: "God is the great companion— the fellow-sufferer who understands" (*PR*, 532). Orthodoxy exempted the deity from change and sorrow. Whitehead's heresy, which many think is the theology that will in the future triumph, is a fresh correction, paradoxical in traditional terms, but marked by its own coherence.

It is as true to say that God is permanent and the World fluent, as that the World
is permanent and God is fluent. (PR, 528)

And the same for one and many, and all the other ways used to separate
the world's categories from God's categories.

God's role is not the combat of productive force with productive force, of
destructive force with destructive force; it lies in the patient operation of the
overpowering rationality of his conceptual harmonization. He does not create
the world, he saves it: or, more accurately, he is *the poet of the world, with tender
patience leading it by his vision of truth, beauty, and goodness.* (PR, 525–26, italics
added)

Whitehead's religious philosophy is, in conclusion, a myth of the world
creating values because it responds to a cosmic artist. Some have called it
"the great analogy": that man creates his works, such as civilization, as
God creates the order of the world.

Is God then not only a ground of order and principle of order, but the
model of all the orders we have studied, rhythm, series, harmony, hierarchy, balance, all as perfectly fused as possible? This is not developed, but
each mode of order is appropriate to the divine nature, and if there is one
actuality, His mode of actuality would be the mingling of the orders to
achieve completeness.

Creation and Entropy:
Order Out of Chaos or Chaos Out of Order

The ground of hope in the process is that there are inexhaustible
possibilities, interminable creativity, and God, "upon whose wisdom all
forms of order depend" (*RM,* 160). Whitehead's philosophy of organism
gives us an account of process bringing order out of chaos, and ever-new
order out of old order. But traditional religion warns of the end of the
world. While Whitehead rejected the Apocalypse, with its angry God
sending sinners to hell while a few saints go to heaven, there is a renewal of
the question "how will the world end?" Should the second law of ther-
modynamics be extended to the world? "Apart from the intervention of
God, there could be nothing new in the world and no order in the world.
The course of creation would be *a dead level of ineffectiveness* . . ." (*PR,* 377,
italics added). Does this mean that because there is God there can be no
heat death of the solar system? God then means the triumph of good over

evil, where "evil" is defined as "the balance and intensity progressively excluded by the cross currents of incompatibility" (*PR*, 377).

The philosophy of organism stresses creativity, process from possibility to actuality, and progress. But there is real evil: destructiveness, "slighter occasions of actuality," and decline. If the adventure is downward as well as upward, and the path of decay is "inevitable," what hope is there? In *Religion in the Making* the conclusion is that although the world is "physically wasting, on the other side it is spiritually ascending" (*RM*, 160). The difficulty here is that the only hope would be the preservation of past achievements in the consequent nature of God, and we must question whether in this system God can be conceived as purely spiritual. If all actuality is bipolar, and God is no exception to the categoreal necessity, how can this be? If God has a physical aspect, then he too must decay. The Cosmology requires "the basis of all religions . . . the dynamic effort of the World passing into everlasting unity, and of the static majesty of God's vision, accomplishing its purpose of completion by absorption of the World's multiplicity of effort" (*PR*, 529–30).

Whitehead is clear that there is no scientific answer to the question "What may I hope?" Evolution, for example, gives an account that is inadequate to the development of civilized progress. When we face "the spectacle of a finite system running down—losing its activities and its varieties," we can appeal to "some tendency upwards, in a contrary direction to the aspect of physical decay." There is purpose and appetition, as in achievement of beauty. The conclusion of the *Function of Reason* put hope in "this reign of Reason," and this may be an alternative to the statements that grounds all hope in God. Rather than speculative, the validity is empirical: "In our experience we find appetition, effecting a final causation towards ideal ends which lie outside the mere physical tendency" (*FR*, 89).

In conclusion, is the philosophy of Whitehead ultimately based on argument, or on intuition, or on faith? The argument for God and Reason is that "mere blind appetition would be the product of chance and lead nowhere" (*FR*, 89). The intuition is that "there is a discrimination of appetitions according to a rule of fitness." Whitehead admits that "this reign of Reason is vascillating, vague, and dim" but because of experience insists that "it is there." What we can know is a "counter-tendency which converts the decay of one order into the birth of its successor" (*FR*, 90).

Whitehead did not consider the question "Why not nothing?" in answer to the ultimate whence. But what of the ultimate whither? Why should not Reason, God, Forms, Creativity all return to nothing? The expression of "speculative imagination" must be considered an act of faith. The final word rests hope upon the system of order:

The present type of order in the world has arisen from an unimaginable past, and it will find its grave in an unimaginable future. There remain the inexhaustible realm of abstract forms, and creativity, with its shifting character ever determined afresh, by its own creatures and God, upon whose wisdom all forms of order depend. (*RM*, 160)

Notes and References

Preface

1. Alfred North Whitehead, *Process and Reality* (New York, 1929), p. 4.
2. George Santayana, *The Letters of George Santayana,* ed. Daniel Cory (New York: Charles Scribner's Sons, 1955), pp. 248, 326–31; cf. p. 385.
3. Paul G. Kuntz, *The Concept of Order* (Seattle: University of Washington Press, 1968), p. xxxiii.

Chapter One

1. The "Personal" part of *Essays in Science and Philosophy* adds up to fifty pages, but the "Education" part of the same book, added to the seven essays already published in *The Aims of Education,* is three times the length. From its earlier English printing, as *The Organisation of Thought,* there were two others not reprinted in the American version, "The Principles of Mathematics in Relation to Elementary Teaching" and "A Polytechnic in War-Time." It is typical of Whitehead, who did not regard himself as an important person, to devote only a fraction of the space to himself in contrast to education, to which he devoted his life.
2. *The Aims of Education* (New York, 1949), p. 29, italics added. Further references will be abbreviated in text *AE,* followed by page number.
3. *Introduction to Mathematics* (rev. ed., New York, 1958), p. 121. Further references will be abbreviated in text *IM,* followed by page number.
4. *Science and the Modern World* (New York, 1926), p. ix. Further references will be abbreviated in text *SMW,* followed by page number.
5. *Essays in Science and Philosophy* (London, 1948), p. 74. Further references will be abbreviated in text *ESP,* followed by page number.
6. *The Organisation of Thought: Educational and Scientific* (London, 1917, 1929), p. 114. In contrast to science is the preference "that thought find its origin in some legend of those great twin brethren, the Cock and Bull." This is omitted from *AE,* 111.
7. *Universal Algebra* (Cambridge, 1898), p. 19. Further references will be abbreviated in text *UA,* followed by page number.
8. *Symbolism, Its Meaning and Effect* (New York, 1927), p. 88. Further references will be abbreviated in text *S,* followed by page number.

Chapter Two

1. Plato, *Sophist* 252 D, 253, *ESP,* 238; see below, Ch. 6, note 7.

2. Aristotle, *Metaphysics* 986a: the Greek says literally "numbers, we have said, [are?] the whole 'ouranon.'" Why not read this that numbers are aspects of the whole universe?

3. Werner Jaeger, *Paideia,* Vol. I (Oxford: Blackwell, 1939), Ch. 9, "Philosophical Speculation: the Discovery of World-Order," pp. 150–84.

4. Biblical references abound in Whitehead and are nearly always to the King James Version and therefore will be cited from this classic. The references are as commonly by book, chapter, and verse.

5. Bertrand Russell, *The Principles of Mathematics,* 2d ed. (London: George Allen & Unwin, 1937)

6. No finer introductions to the logic of relations exist than those of Whitehead, particularly the articles, some with Russell, in *Encyclopaedia Britannica,* 11th ed. Whitehead's articles are republished in *ESP.* They may best be reinforced by Bertrand Russell, *Introduction to Mathematical Philosophy* (London: Allen & Unwin, 1918), "The Definition of Order," and by Josiah Royce, *Logical Essays* (Dubuque, Iowa: Wm. C. Brown Co, 1951). For a continuance of the philosophical importance, see Paul G. Kuntz, *The Concept of Order* (Seattle: University of Washington Press, 1968). The next step is to read further in Whitehead's *Principia Mathematica.* From this three-volume masterpiece there is a short paperback of the early part.

7. F. S. C. Northrop and Mason W. Gross, *Alfred North Whitehead: An Anthology* (New York, 1953), pp. 11–82.

8. *PM* here and hereafter will refer to *Principia Mathematica,* with Bertrand Russell. Cambridge: At the University Press, Vols. I–III, 1910–1913.

9. *Modes of Thought* (New York, 1938), pp. 92–93, with words added in brackets [ ], pp. 92–93. Further references will be abbreviated in text *MT,* with page number.

10. *Adventures of Ideas* (New York, 1933), p. 196. Further references will be abbreviated in text *AI,* followed by page number.

Chapter Three

1. The importance of Hume for Whitehead can be grasped from *Science and the Modern World* (*SMW,* 75–76, 83f); also in *Process and Reality* (*PR,* 77–78, 114, 129, 132–33, 140, 144, 172–75, 179–81, 187–89, 196, 198–217, 221–54, 259, 263–67, 270, 272, 370–71, 380–82, 389, 480–82, 497, 520–21); and *Adventures of Ideas* (*AI,* 159–60, 225, 236–37, 283–89). Most of the secondary literature is concerned with causality solely, and whether Whitehead "answered" Hume. In contrast, see Kuntz, "Hume's Metaphysics: A New Theory of Order," *Religious Studies* 12 (1976):401–28.

2. *Process and Reality,* pp. 111–12. 172, 236–37. Further references will be abbreviated in text *PR,* followed by page number.

3. *Religion in the Making* (New York, 1927) discusses this contrast most fully and will be considered in Chapter 7. Further references will be abbreviated in text *RM,* followed by page number.

4. *On Mathematical Concepts of the Material World,* in Northrop and Gross, *An Anthology,* p. 11. Further references will be abbreviated in text *MCMW,* followed by page number.

5. *An Enquiry Concerning Principles of Natural Knowledge,* 2d ed. (Cambridge, 1925), p. v. Further references will be abbreviated in text *PNK,* followed by page number.

6. *The Concept of Nature* (Cambridge, 1920) p. 2, italics added. Further references will be abbreviated in text *CN,* followed by page number.

7. *The Principle of Relativity* (Cambridge, 1922), p. 66. Further references will be abbreviated in text *R,* followed by page number.

Chapter Four

1. *The Function of Reason* (Princeton, N.J., 1929), pp. 33–34. Further references will be abbreviated in text *FR,* followed by page number.

Chapter Five

1. David Hume, *Dialogues Concerning Natural Religion,* ed. Norman Kemp Smith (Indianapolis: Bobbs-Merrill Co., n.d.) Philo in Part XII includes among orderly processes "the rotting of a turnip." See Paul G. Kuntz, "Hume's Metaphysics: A New Theory of Order," *Religious Studies* 12(1976):401–28.

2. Karl Marx, *Theses on Feuerbach,* in *Collected Works* (Moscow: 1962), 2:405.

3. Marion Leathers Daniels Kuntz, "Harmony and the Heptaplomeres of Jean Bodin," *Journal of the History of Philosophy* 12, no. 1 (January 1974):31–41.

Chapter Six

1. *PR,* 30–42 is initially less intelligible than the notes 42–55, and particularly "Some Derivative Notions," pp. 46–54.

2. On the Nameless Tao in Chinese thought, see Wing-Tsit Chan, *A Source Book in Chinese Philosophy* (Princeton, N.J.: Princeton University Press, 1963), pp. 139–76.

3. On the undifferentiated in Indian thought, see Sarvepalli Radhakrishnan and Charles A. Moore, *A Source Book in Indian Philosophy* (Princeton, N.J.: Princeton University Press, 1957) on Brahman, pp. 38–96, 506–71.

4. Marion L. Kuntz, *Guillaume Postel: Prophet of the Restitution of All Things: His Life and Thought* (The Hague: Martinus Nijhoff, 1981).

5. H. W. Fowler, *A Dictionary of Modern English Usage* (Oxford: Clarendon Press, 1926), p. 70.

6. The literal statement from Lucretius is "nullam rem e nihilo gigni diuinitus umquam" (T. Lucreti Cari, *De Rerum Natura Libri Sex,* ed. William Ellery Leonard and Stanley Barney Smith [Madison: University of Wisconsin Press, 1968], p. 219(150). The first law is "that nothing is ever begotten of nothing." Cyril Bailey, *Lucretius on the Nature of Things* (Oxford: Clarendon Press), pp. 31–32.

7. On Hegel's 272 categories, see William L. Reese, *Dictionary of Philosophy and Religion: Eastern and Western Thought* (New Jersey: Humanities Press, 1980), pp. 211–15. On the infinite number of categories, see Morton White, *Toward Reunion in Philosophy,* (New York: Atheneum, 1963) Ch. 5, "Categories and Postulates," pp. 81–96.

8. It is very significant that Whitehead should have selected the principles that account for "life and motion." This is cosmology, and Whitehead downplayed what are called the categories of Plato, given as "being, motion, rest, identity, difference," the highest kinds or most universal forms. Whitehead made much of the science of universal forms (Sophist 253) but not of the five kinds (Sophist 255). Although we should question whether Whitehead is completely correct that "Plato left no system of metaphysics," we can see his reason: the purely general would apply only to "a static world." That is, it is the subcategories of motion that account for our world' and not "being, rest, identity, difference." Given the importance attached by Whitehead to "the mingling of forms" (Ch. 2, note 1, reference to Sophist 252D, 253, *ESP,* 129) we might expect the philosopher to discuss the five "classes." One explanation might be that Whitehead was more the mathematical physicist and therefore more interested in Plato's Timaeus.

Chapter Seven

1. There is a curious reversal of attitude in the cases of Russell and Whitehead. The early Whitehead had nothing to say on religion, and only with *Science and the Modern World* gained a favorable reassessment of religion and a doctrine of God. The early Russell had published "A Free Man's Worship," and there is a very positive estimate of the value of Worship, Acquiescence, and Love in "The Essence of Religion." This was published in the *Hibbert Journal* (October 1912), and is now available in Robert E. Egner and Lester E. Denonn, eds., *The Basic Writings of Bertrand Russell 1903–1959* (London: George Allen & Unwin, 1961), pp. 565–76. By the time Whitehead published *Science and the Modern World* (1926), Russell in the hostile mood of "Why I Am Not a Christian" (1927) (ibid., pp. 585–97) reviewed Whitehead's book under the title "Is Science Superstitious?" (see Russell, *Sceptical Essays,* Ch. 3, pp. 35–44).

2. Ewert H. Cousins, "Truth in St. Bonaventura," *Proceedings of the American Catholic Philosophical Association* 43 (1969): 204–10, and *Process Theology: Basic Writings* New York: Newman Press, 1971).

3. Arnold Toynbee, *A Study of History,* abridgment by D. C. Somervell (New York: Oxford University Press, 1947), and *An Historian's Approach to Religion* (London: Oxford University Press, 1956).

4. *A New English Dictionary* (Oxford: Clarendon Press, 1933), Vol. 10 "Truth," p. 402; "Truth," pp. 435–36.

5. See Ch. 6, note 2.

Selected Bibliography

PRIMARY SOURCES

Adventures of Ideas. New York: Macmillan Company, 1933; Cambridge: At the University Press, 1933 (these editions have the same pagination); Harmondsworth, Middlesex, and Baltimore: Penguin Books, 1933, and subsequently, the New American Library.

The Aims of Education. New York: The New American Library, 1949. Originally, *The Organisation of Thought*. London: Williams and Norgate, 1929, and new edition, New York: Macmillan, 1950.

The Concept of Nature. Cambridge: At the University Press, 1920; Ann Arbor: University of Michigan Press, 1957.

An Enquiry Concerning the Principles of Natural Knowledge. Cambridge: At the University Press, 1919; 2d ed., 1925.

Essays in Science and Philosophy. London: Rider and Company, 1948; New York: Philosophical Library, 1948. There is a 1947 edition from the latter, but this lacks "Uniformity and Contingency"; Wisdom Library, under title *Science and Philosophy*.

The Function of Reason. Princeton, N.J.: Princeton University Press, 1929; also Oxford University Press, and Boston: Beacon Press.

Introduction to Mathematics. Home University Library, originally 1911; rev. ed., Oxford: Oxford University Press, 1958 (Galaxy); London: Williams and Norgate; New York: H. Holt, 1945, J. H. C. Whitehead, ed., Twelfth Impression, 1948.

On Mathematical Concepts of the Material World. In F. S. C. Northrop and Mason W. Gross, eds. *Alfred North Whitehead: An Anthology*. New York: Macmillan, 1953, pp. 11–82.

Modes of Thought. New York: The Macmillan Company, 1938, and subsequently; Cambridge: At the University Press, 1938 (these editions have the same pagination) also (Capricorn).

With Bertrand Russell. *Principia Mathematica*. Cambridge: At the University Press. Vol. 1, 1910; Vol 2, 1912; Vol. 3, 1913; 2d ed., 1925–1927. There is a back edition by Cambridge University Press, 1962, *Principia Mathematica* to *56.

The Principle of Relativity. Cambridge: At the University Press, 1922.

Process and Reality. New York: Macmillan Co., 1929; Cambridge: At the University Press, 1929 (Harper Torchbooks).

Religion in the Making. New York: Macmillan Co.; Cambridge: At the University Press, 1927 (Meridian Books).

Science and the Modern World. Cambridge: At the University Press, 1926; New York: Macmillan Co., 1925, 1926 (Mentor Book, the New American Library, 1948).

Symbolism, Its Meaning and Effect. New York: Macmillan Co., 1927, and subsequently; Cambridge: At the University Press, 1928 (Capricorn Books).

Universal Algebra. Cambridge: At the University Press, 1898.

SECONDARY SOURCES

The most complete bibliography of secondary sources, along with primary sources, is Barry A. Woodbridge, ed. *Alfred North Whitehead: A Primary-Secondary Bibliography.* Bowling Green, Ohio: Philosophy Documentation Center, 1977. The primary and secondary works, without counting reviews, number almost two thousand (1868). This work analyzes the topics in each article and book and is admirably indexed.

There are four valuable collections of essays: Otis H. Lee, ed. *Essays for Alfred North Whitehead.* New York: Longmans, Green, 1936; Paul A. Schilpp, ed. *The Philosophy of Alfred North Whitehead.* Evanston and Chicago: Northwestern University Press, 1st ed., 1941; New York: Tudor Publishing Co., 2d ed., 1951; Ivor Leclerc, ed. *The Relevance of Whitehead: Philosophical Essays in Commemoration of the Birth of Alfred North Whitehead.* London: George Allen & Unwin; New York: Humanities Press, 1961; George L. Kline. *Alfred North Whitehead: Essays on His Philosophy.* Englewood Cliffs, N.J.: Prentice-Hall, 1963.

Special issues of journals also give a variety of interpretations. Lewis S. Ford, ed. "Special Issue on Whitehead." *Southern Journal of Philosophy* 7, no. 4 (Winter 1969–70); Robert C. Whittemore, ed. *Studies in Whitehead's Philosophy. Tulane Studies in Philosophy* 10 (1961), and two issues of *Tulane Studies* devoted to Process Philosophy: 23 (1974) and 24 (1975).

Christian, William A. *An Interpretation of Whitehead's Metaphysics,* New Haven: Yale University Press, 1959. The most thorough study of "God and the World," on the basis of "Actual Occasions" and "Eternal Objects."

Emmet, Dorothy. *Whitehead's Philosophy of Organism.* London: Macmillan, 1932; 2d ed., 1966. An engaging study of the Platonic aspects of Whitehead's philosophy.

Hall, David L. *The Civilization of Experience: A Whiteheadian Theory of Culture.* New York: Fordham Univeristy Press, 1973.

Hartshorne, Charles. *Whitehead's Philosophy: Selected Essays 1935–1970.* Lincoln: University of Nebraska Press, 1972.

———, and Reese, William L. *Philosophers Speak of God.* Chicago: University of Chicago Press, 1953.

Johnson, Allison H. *Whitehead's American Essays in Social Philosophy.* New York: Harper, 1959. With an interpretation and selection of essays.

———, ed. *Whitehead: The Interpretation of Science.* Indianapolis: Bobbs-Merrill, 1961.

Lawrence, Nathaniel M. *Alfred North Whitehead: A Primer of His Philosophy.* Boston: Twayne Publishers, 1974. The most balanced study of the whole position.

———. *Whitehead's Philosophical Development: A Critical History of the Background of Process and Reality.* Berkeley: University of California Press, 1956. Most helpful on Whitehead's philosophy of nature.

Leclerc, Ivor. *Whitehead's Metaphysics: An Introductory Exposition.* London: George Allen and Unwin, 1958. The most thorough on Whitehead in context of the Aristotelian tradition.

Lowe, Victor. *Understanding Whitehead.* Baltimore: Johns Hopkins Press, 1962, 1966. The most comprehensive study told in stages of development.

Mays, Wolfe. *The Philosophy of Whitehead.* New York: Macmillan, 1959.

Palter, Robert M. *Whitehead's Philosophy of Science.* Chicago: University of Chicago Press, 1960, 1970. The best general commentary on Whitehead as a scientist and philosopher of science.

Sherburne, Donald W. *A Key to Whitehead's "Process and Reality."* New York: Macmillan, 1966.

———. *A Whiteheadian Aesthetic.* New Haven, Conn.: Yale University Press, 1961.

Index

References are to pages. The symbol "/" is used for contrast, opposition, or exclusion, as mind/matter, order/disorder, true/false. The relationship is to be considered sometimes symmetrical, as equivalent to matter/mind, but sometimes asymmetrical, since disorder is the absence of order, and without order there could be no disorder. Sometimes the relationship is to be considered as thesis and antithesis, as order to chaos, but at other times as synthesizable as order/freedom or order/progress.

Darwin, Charles, 73, 76, 82

Democritus, 81, 93, 109, 110, 115

Descartes, René, 75, 115, 124

Dewey, John, 47

dialectic, *see* thesis, antithesis and synthesis

dignity of man in nature, 73

dipolarity, 141, *see also* opposites

disorder, a form of order, 58; —not necessarily bad, 86; —and order fundamental to the universe, 119; in experience or flux of impressions, 29, 77; jingling expressions of, 95, *see also* chaos

dogmatism, why bad, 94

dualism, see bifurcation

dualism, modern/ancient, 98

dualisms, overcome, 9

ecology, 59, 74

Einstein, 35, 42, 59, *see also* Relativity, Theory of

emotions, 64, 66

empirical method in metaphysics, 95, 99

entropy, problem of, 142–44

essences, *see* eternal objects

Eternal objects, 21–26, 39; hierarchy of, 25–26

ethics, 74–77, 120, *see also* good/evil

events, 22–23, 54–55, 56; spatially and temporally related, 36, 39, 79

evil, problem of, solved, 135–39

evolutionary ethics or social Darwinism, 76

evolutionary order, 73

existence, categories of, *see* categories, four types of, *see also* what

experience, process from disorder towards order, 29

explanation, categories of, *see* categories of explanation

extension, 37–38; relations between events, 37–39

extensions, composed of extensionless points and moments? (Zeno), 60

extensive, abstaction, method of, 38

fact, public/private, 116, 117; stubborn, 65

fallacy of misplaced concreteness, 47, 49; of perfect order, 86, 95, *see* one perfect order, *see also* utopia; of simple location, 47

fate, remorseless working of things, 44

feeling, 66

feelings as vectors, 121, *see also* vector

final cause, 119; shared by God with all actual entities which are characterized by self-causation, 122

flux, philosophy of, why philosophy of process not a, 93

force, *see* competition/cooperation

formative elements, 100

forms, Platonic, 98, *see also* eternal objects

freedom and purpose, 52

Galileo, 42, 45, 140

geometry, science of dimensional order, 41

God, 7, 10, 15, 16, 25, 27, 32–33, 57, 58, 73, 74, 80, 81, 84, 85, 87, 89, 100–107, 110, 116, 122–44, 133, *see also* Allah, Alpha and Omega, Being Itself, Brahma, Creator, Jehovah, prime mover; aesthetic order, immanence of, 136, *see also* cosmos, belief in, *see also* truth, beauty, goodness; completeness of modes of order characterizing, 142; a formative element but not a category, 99; ground of